CONFLICT at the BORDER

—true tales of a U.S. Customs border officer!

Words and illustrations by

Charles S. Park

Golden West Publishers

Front and back cover designed by Bruce Fischer/The Art Studio

The events recorded in this book are reconstructed for greater entertainment value and, in any case, represent only the author's version of them. Names pre-reported in border histories are real; the others are fictitious, nor are any illustrations deliberate caricaturization of any individual.

Library of Congress Cataloging-in-Publication Data

Park, Charles S.,
Conflict at the border: true tales of a U.S. Customs border officer / by Charles S. Park.

1. Mexican-American Border Region—Social life and customs—Anecdotes. 2. Park, Charles S.—Anecdotes. 3. U.S. Customs Service—Officials and employees—Anecdotes. 4. Customs administration—Mexican-American Border Region—Anecdotes. I. Title.
F787.P37 1989 979—dc 19 89-1923 CIP
ISBN 0-914846-41-8

Printed in the United States of America

Golden West Publishers
4113 N. Longview Ave.
Phoenix, AZ 85014, USA
(602) 265-4392

Contents

Introduction

Centuries before Phillip St. George Cooke led the Mormon Battalion out of Santa Fe to find a southern route to San Diego, the Indians occupied the land he would traverse. Then came the Spaniards, followed by the Mexicans, and finally, the Americans, who in the beginning used Cooke's Wagon Road to get to the California gold.

Trouble was, the Road was in Mexico, and Mexico and the United States were at war. Hostilities over, the Treaty of Guadalupe Hidalgo put the northern boundary of Mexico principally at the Rio Grande and Gila Rivers, but still did not put the Road in the U.S.A.

The Gadsden Purchase did that in 1853. More, it brought into the United States people who spoke Indian dialects and Spanish-speaking Catholics, together with their respective cultures.

Nothing changed abruptly and 135 years later there are still Spanish-speaking Catholics, people who speak the Indian dialects, the same food, music, and way of life.

Some of the folks who now live between the Gila River and the International Line think the border should have stayed at the Gila. Some in the area talk about seceding from the rest of Arizona to form their own State — the Fifty-first.

At least one reason for secession is a difference in the cultures of people who live in places like Phoenix, Chandler, Florence, Prescott, Paradise Valley and Scottsdale, to mention but a few, and those who live in communities with names like Sentinel Peak (Tucson), Walnut Trees (Nogales), White Gold (Oro Blanco), Squash (Calabasas), Tres Bellotas (Three Acorn Trees), Place Where Corn Grows (Sonoita), and Pigeon Droppings (Palomitas). Anglos who have moved into this informal Fifty-first tend to group together, as many Americans tend to do in foreign lands, forming enclaves such as Green Valley, Tubac, and Rio Rico.

This was not true in earlier days when U.S. Government employees came to regulate commerce and immigration across the new border.

Most of these were truly individualists. There was Drinkwater, the first Customs Inspector in this region below Tucson, who was said to be more partial to *mescal* than he was to H_20; Lt. Britton Davis of the U.S. Army, who conspired with the Apache, Geronimo, to beat the Customs Service out of its just duties; Mounted Customs Patrolman Luke Short, a name well-known to *aficionados* of Western history; and Jeff Milton, more of the same, who was variously the first Chinese Inspector, an Immigration officer, and a Customs man.

Other border officers and civilians of the Fifty-first State may not be as well known, but are easily as individual.

In this book of episodes that took place at or were related to the International Line, some of these characters are introduced..

Although none mentioned is a fictitious person, names as well as some identifying details in the collection of happenings are changed in order not to cause unintentional embarrassment to anyone. These occurrences as written represent the author's observation of them and not necessarily that of other witnesses.

For the benefit of those who will be helped by it, there is a translation of Spanish words used in the text at the end of the book.

Charles L. Park

He Put Nogales on the Map!

Her personal nickname for him was Rayme. Others called him Bill. Neither Ada nor Rayme dreamed that they would one day become an important part of the history of the Mexican border.

Ada MacPherson was the most beautiful girl at Iowa State. It was no wonder that her puzzled father, the conservative Judge, said to her: "You could have your choice of any man at the school or outside of it. Why choose one who is your social and intellectual inferior?"

She was a dutiful daughter who respected her father, and valued his opinion, but this time she said, "He won't always be."

He was only 19 when he graduated. He found work in Colorado, where he was over-qualified for his first job: brush-cutting for a survey party, which was about as low as you could get when your degree was in civil engineering.

A burly, lazy co-worker thought that because of his ferocious attack on growth in the path of the chain and transit, and his eagerness to learn, Rayme was trying to make points with the bosses. Inevitably there was a fight in which Rayme took a beating. Two days later, still aching from it, he jumped the other man, saw he wasn't going to win, grabbed a pickhandle and floored him with it, thus demonstrating that he was not one to be under-estimated.

Five weeks later he was head surveyor of that party. It was as a promising young engineer he returned to Iowa where he and Ada were married.

One of his attributes was total confidence in himself. When the political struggle over the routing of a railroad in 1872 put him and others like him out of work, he took over management of an estate, then bought a newspaper in Cimarron, New Mexico, where his outspoken crusade against corrupt officials brought threats on his life.

Ada finally said, "Rayme, I hate this savage land."

As though her words had sparked violence, a man on a sweat-streaked horse pounded into their yard. Out of the dust of his arrival burst another rider who shot once, and Rayme's printer died on their doorstep while their three-year old daughter, munching a piece of bread and sugar, looked on in horror as blue-bottle flies settled on the bloody corpse.

The killing was linked to Clay Allison, who had just supervised the wrecking of Rayme's shop on behalf of those opposed to his views. The sheriff was reluctant to go after Allison, well-known shootist.

Ada found Rayme, who had a phobia about unloaded guns, carefully unwrapping his from the piece of red flannel he had stored it away in, out of reach of their little girl.

Ada cried, "Rayme! What are you doing?"

"Going after Allison," he said. But he had heard the plaintive, desperate note in her voice and realized there was more involved here than *machismo* or the avenging of a friend and employee.

"Start packing," he said. "We'll find some more railroads to build somewhere"

They did. Glorieta Pass, La Veta Pass, Raton Pass, and as a single-handed representative of the Santa Fe he beat the Denver and Rio Grande to the coveted Royal Gorge route to Leadville, tricking 100 armed men in the process.

When that battle was over, Santa Fe's General Strong presented Rayme with a gold-mounted Winchester Repeating Rifle. Characteristically, when he accepted it he worked the lever to clear the chamber of this presumably "unloaded" gun.

There were more railroads to build and he went on to build them. In 1882 he finished one from the Port of Guaymas, Sonora, on the West Coast of Mexico to the International Line. Pretty Ada had the honor and pleasure of tapping the little silver spike into place at the joining-up ceremony with the railroad line down from Benson, Arizona. There was a celebration later in the Santa Rita Hotel in Calabasas, and Ada smiled with pride at her husband, at ease in hat and tails. He had come a long way from the college boy her father had referred to as her "social and intellectual inferior."

A year or so later he was investigating another possible route for a railroad in a wild and rugged place near Aguascalientes, Mexico, and entered a two-seated hack to find himself staring down the barrel of a 30-30 carbine that was leaning against the back of the driver's seat. He promptly asked the driver to move it.

"It's not loaded," the driver said, but complied.

The ends of the lines had become tangled around the stock so he jerked them to free them.

The unarmed man who had faced a hundred others with loaded weapons in the battle for the Royal Gorge died under the hammer of an "unloaded" gun, the kind he feared the most.

One of the two principal streets in Nogales, Arizona, bears the family name of that man who helped put the border city on the map: William Raymond Morley.

The Concordia

Where Morley Avenue ends and Mexico begins there ought to be a commemorative plaque inscribed with the names of the famous and not so famous who had walked between the aging tufa columns to pass, look into, or enter the now defunct Concordia *cantina.*

It was only about 30 fast steps into Sonora for a thirsty man, and when the government closed down the Gate for 12 hours a day and all day Sundays to help offset a budgetary deficiency, hundreds of deceased dedicated clients of the Concordia caused a major earthquake on Cemetery Hill as they whirled in their graves.

There was so much history of the Southwest Frontier discussed in the Concordia of a quiet evening that if it had all been taped and stored there, even that spacious saloon would not have been able to contain it all.

The Concordia corner should be placed on the list of Arizona's Historical Sites even though it is in Sonora, Mexico.

Only a few are left to mourn its demise. Certainly none of the *domperos,* those unfortunates who existed by competing with the crows and coyotes for choice morsels of trash and garbage at the city landfill, and hiked thrice daily to the Concordia where they could temporarily ease their lot, for a dime a shot, with *mescal* or *sotol,* and partake of whatever *botana* was being offered. The round trip was three miles, so they got plenty of exercise.

Long before surveyors arrived to plot future roads, parched Americans found the shortest routes to the border. Their pounding feet, the hoofs of their horses, the iron tires on their wagon wheels, tamped down the foundations of what would become Interstate 19 and State Highways 82 and 89 to converge upon the Concordia.

The precise date of entry of this all-night spa into border history is vague in the few remaining memories, but somewhere in the archives of the capital city of Hermosillo, Sonora, or in the files of the Pimeria Alta Historical Society in Nogales, Arizona, there must be a record of when the first entrepreneur poured the first drink on this spot.

The Concordia was shaped architecturally like a slice of pizza, geometrically like a horizontal isosceles triangle. Its broad front, the base facing the border, held two louvred doors that never stopped swinging.

Inside were two bars. One ran along an edge of the slice of pizza, one along the other. Both almost met in a one-seater community toilet—not that many women used it, or were even welcome in the Concordia, for the saloon was primarily a man's meeting place.

A constant stream of water flowed through a mossy spit trough between the brass rail and the front of the bar. Behind the bar hung an ancient painting of a nude so faded and yellowed by age that most of the excitement had gone out of it. A century of odors of spilled beer, tequila, and a powerful disinfectant infrequently used in the privy was embedded in the dark woodwork of the bullet-scarred battered bar that was said to have seen service before 1880 in Calabasas, in the dirtfilled cracks of the white tile floor, and sticking to the peeling yellow paint of the moulded tin ceiling.

On hot summer afternoons lazy ceiling fans forced the mingled odors over the swinging doors where they drifted across the border to pollute the pure Arizona air, causing eyes to smart and nostrils to drain as the noxious cloud moved invisibly north along Morley Avenue like tear gas on the wind up from Mexico.

It was a policy of the establishment that those few ladies who entered unescorted could walk in one swinging door, walk as far as the toilet, turn, walk along the other bar and out the other door. If any customer felt so inclined, he could follow her twitching behind to wherever it might lead. The rule tended to keep down violence on the premises.

Returning now to the proposed plaque, files of the border newspapers revealed that Nogales was often on the itinerary of the rich and famous.

To name a few: Harold Bell Wright, Jack Dempsey, Arthur Brisbane, Will Rogers, Gene Tunney, Elliott Roosevelt, Admiral William F. Halsey, Jr., John Foster Dulles, Yvonne de Carlo, Ruth Roman, Victoria Shaw, Roger Smith, Stewart Granger, Jean Simmons, Archie Moore, Ben Ames Williams, Mrs. Gutzum Borgland, Jayne Mansfield, Ambassador Lewis Douglas, Ambassador Raul Castro, "Soapy" Williams, Black Jack Pershing, Pancho Villa, General Douglas MacArthur, Spencer Tracy, John Wayne, Frank Morgan, Van Johnson.

Some of those immortals closer to home but not so nationally known who met evenings at the Concordia to go over the day's events were Bob Long, District Director of Customs; Bill Shane, his Chief Inspector; Sammy Shapiro, merchant; Sam Kolver, jeweler; Max Arnold and Marty Loughman, produce men; John Summey, Postmaster; Johnny George, the international businessman; a host of Customs and Immigration officers, too many others to include in this short report.

Serving drinks to all of these were three *cantineros* who poured tequila by the gallon, soda by the same, and sliced quarters of lime with the accuracy and rapidity of Chinese cooks: taciturn Huero and accommodating Chapo, who also laid out *botana*, often *cahuama* from the Sea of Cortez, along with fresh corn tortillas for those who were hungry as well as thirsty, and Dennis Ryan, who gave up a life time behind bars to become a U.S. Customs Inspector.

As an influential institution the Concordia ranked high, holding a unique position among the differences separating the dwellers in the Gadsden Purchase from those who settled north of the Gila River.

The Fading Tequila Trail

The Treaty of Guadalupe Hidalgo established the Gila River as the northern boundary of Mexico in Arizona. That was changed by the Gadsden Purchase, which altered lives and created novelties like the Concordia. Today, many folks among those residing between the Gila and the present border are vociferous in their argument that the boundary never should have been moved and shout that secession from the rest of the State would form a Fifty-first and make a more perfect Union.

Long-time residents can remember when the Line was staffed by veterans of the Spanish-American War and World War I, many of them near mandatory retirement. Enter young veterans of World War II to try to infuse the old gray Customs bureaucracy with new red blood. Then came the veterans of Korea and Vietnam to introduce the electronic age, but nobody has been able to develop a computer that will ask border crossers: "Are you an American citizen?" and: "What are you bringing?"

If one believes that definitive book about the city of Calabasas by James Cabell Brown, the first Customs Inspector in the Territory was named Drinkwater, of whom it was said he consumed very little of that precious fluid except as chaser for bourbon when beer was unavailable.

Whether or not he set the precedent, if a cross-section of Customs Inspectors in Arizona for the next 100 years or so had been subjected to blood testing, their alcohol level at any given moment would have greatly surpassed the maximum percentage allowable under DUI laws today.

Part of the alcohol problem faced by inspectors stemmed from the proximity of the Concordia Club to the Morley Avenue workplace.

Customs Inspector Stu Hayworth, for example, liked his drinks so much he kept a bottle cooling in the toilet tanks at the Morley Avenue and Grand Avenue *garitas.* He was a small man with a big nose who always walked rapidly, leaning forward as into a high wind.

There was the time he was working at Morley Avenue when a number of all-night revelers spilled out of the Concordia singing contentedly and marching arm-in-arm west along the Mexican side of the international fence behind a quartet of *mariachis.* Such temptation was too much for Hayworth.

Chief Inspector of Customs Randolph Adams and his assistant were leaning against the wall of the Federal Building, taking the morning sum. Neither Adams nor his assistant could see very well, and wore thick glasses to help their vision.

Attracted by the sound of mariachi music, they peered myopically across the border fence, where Hayworth, leaning against a non-existent breeze, was leading the band with a half-full bottle of mescal for baton.

"Tell me," Adams begged, "I'm not seeing what I'm looking at."

Only the fact that he was a good inspector when sober kept Hayworth in active status. Chief Adams remembered when Hayworth, newly established in Nogales, awakened thirsty one night, heard sounds of a party next door and went there hoping for an invitation to come in for a drink. Instead, he was met with rudeness and informed he was out of his jurisdiction. A call for help to subdue the noisy group would not have been effective, for the police chief was among the *groseros.*

Came the dawn and Hayworth searched among the many empty tequila bottles in a GI can awaiting trash collection in front of the neighbor's house where he was pleased to find a receipt for their total on a Concordia bill. A search of Customs records found no notice of duties and internal revenue tax paid, so Hayworth's neighbor found that his earlier rudeness and lack of foresight in leaving Hayworth off the list of invited guests had become exceedingly costly.

Hayworth's memory was elephantine. It took a year and luck before he was able to pin the police chief.

It was customary to give local law enforcement officers courtesy of the port, to wave them through the gates without examination. The chief crossed from Mexico one evening in his official car, exchanged pleasantries with the inspectors on duty and drove on to pull in behind the police station a block away. Here he opened the trunk lid and began to transfer the load of liquor he had smuggled over the border to his personal car.

Stu Hayworth just happened to drive into the parking lot behind him.

The Volstead Act created a definite hardship for many in the U.S., but there was never any prohibition for residents of the United States who could reach Mexico. The Concordia, for instance, never closed its swinging doors until its untimely demise.

"Nothing will ever be the same," mourn the few oldsters who remember the Concordia as it was, as they shuffle across the border for their daily *tequilitas* elsewhere, passing that familiar corner where the old saloon used to be where today only the name over the door of a liquor store remains as a reminder of the fading tequila trail.

Shattered Legend

Another Concordia habitue' who warrants space in these columns was *Coronel* Abel Bonillas, retired from the Mexican Army longer than he had served in it.

He was a legend of considerable stature along the border. His reputation as a bad man to cross was so well-known among the citizens that he was no longer crossed by any of them. They knew that he had been, and believed he still could be, a ferocious fighter, in spite of his years.

The old campaigner's image of ferocity was enhanced by the heavy Colt Peacemaker .45 model 1873 hanging along his thigh, which he carried as a perk of his status as an old Federal soldier, as was the starched khaki uniform he habitually wore. His threatening appearance was further advanced by a bushy white mustache that came to waxed needle points far out on each side of his lined brown face, like the head ornaments of a Texas longhorn.

Whenever the coronel was disturbed, which was rarely, because of his reputed propensity for violence, the points of the mustache began to quiver until the disturber got the message and retreated before being engulfed in a mutilating, possibly lethal, explosion.

He lived in the Abadie Hotel above the Concordia and it was not unusual for him to be in his usual place at the scarred bar on a dreary warm Sunday at three a.m., finishing off the second of his normal quota of two liters of mescal per day, when in walked a lady of the night with shifty hips who winked at him and walked out again. He downed his drink and shoved away from the bar.

He was unaware that the object of his sudden desire also winked at Rodney Whitney, a cowboy newcomer to the frontier, a lean mean product of West Texas, moodily downing Straight American straight in an effort to prepare himself to be in the saddle at the Bar Lazy S at the rapidly nearing sunrise.

Whitney and Bonillas met for the first time at the swinging door. The cowboy gave the old gentleman a body block that hurled his ancient bones crashing into the bar and was long gone before Bonillas got his arm out of the spit trough and his feet untangled from the brass rail.

The points of his mustache quivering dangerously, he roared out into Internatinal Street, which was quiet except for the distant clatter of the round rock that Bulla, a nocturnal songbird about whom more will be said later, was tossing down the street in front of himself.

The coronel absorbed and discarded that sound as he did the other familiar night noises of this border city: distant mariachi

music, the clatter and rattle of an old *tranvia* far down Avenida Obregon, the muted voices of the U.S. Customs and Immigration officers in front of the garita at the Morley Avenue gate trying to keep each other awake.

No noise emanated from the dark open mouth of Elias Street as the suspicious, enraged old infantryman charged to its end and back, breathing flame and belching steam, and did not see Whitney and the *puta* getting it on standing up in the shadowed vestibule of the curio store next door to La Caverna.

When Bonillas re-entered the Concordia, Chapo, the jug-eared little graveyard bartender, shoved a new bottle of mescal across the bar, nodding in solemn agreement and shuddering as Bonillas described in horrible detail what he would do to Whitney if he ever saw him again.

Taking a strong, nerve-calming pull at the new bottle, the coronel headed for the single-seater co-ed water-closet to make room for more fluid.

Chapo fiddled with the bottles on the backbar until a voice behind him rasped, "Hey, barty, gimme one of them bottles of American Straight to go."

Before horrified Chapo could get the bottle into Whitney's hand, Bonillas stumbled from the toilet buttoning his fly, an effort he totally abandoned when he saw Whitney, while the points of his mustache whirled like twin propellors.

He drew his ancient hogleg.

Whitney, trying to distract him, said, "Fly's open, soldier."

Bonillas squalled, "And I'm about to de-fly you, *gallo*."

He thumbed the hammer back, jerked the trigger. Chapo leaped out of the line of fire. Whitney stood frozen in shocked disbelief.

Bonillas re-thumbed the hammer, fired again. There was a crash of broken glass, a rush of gushing mescal and the continued roar of the ancient revolver as Coronel Bonillas fanned the hammer in furious motion.

The silence was absolute after the last bullet left the red-hot barrel. Whitney held out his hand without turning, Chapo slapped the bottle of bourbon into it, Whitney said, "Beats me what a few drinks will do to some fellers," dropped a shower of coins on the bar, and trotted for the safety of Morley Avenue and the United States.

He left Coronel Abel Bonillas (Ret.) staring at the abrupt end of his careeer as a border legend of terror and mayhem: six fresh crotch-high bullet holes in the battered front of the old mahogany bar and not a single drop of Whitney blood.

The Dirty Rat and the Mad Dog

Another renowned border shootist was Jimmy Gleason. His father was a huge man who had lost his front teeth in a saloon brawl and had them all replaced with gold ones. Goldy Gleason died with his boots on in another saloon, disappointed in Jimmy, who was going to be a runt.

Jimmy made up for his lack of size by becoming as big a brawler as his father had been. But he never fought with anyone smaller than himself, and he never lost a fight, even though it might take him days, weeks, or even months to win.

One of his notable exploits is the summer day he rode up to the border saloon on the Mexican side at Sasabe to find its few patrons in the road outside, nursing assorted lumps and contusions, listening to the crash of breaking glass and thrown furniture from inside the bar.

Little Jimmy had been working on the Bamoa ranch below Pitiquito, Sonora. It had been a long, dry, dusty three-day ride and he had worked up an over-sized thirst.

"What gives?" he asked.

"Big mean man in there with a big mean gun," they said. "He run us out."

"How big a gun?" Jimmy asked.

"New model Remington .44 six-shooter," they said.

"Hell," Jimmy said as he slid off his horse, "all you need is a bigger gun."

He jerked the .30-30 carbine from the saddle scabbard and walked through the door shooting. He didn't hit anything but the backbar mirror and a few bottles of mescal, but he caught the rowdy's attention. He threw down his gun and up his hands.

Jimmy wanted to get into the Customs Service as a Mounted Patrolman badly. He would do anything to get a job with them. He wanted to wear one of those round badges and Black Jack Pershing campaign hats and lay out on the Line watching for smugglers.

Captain George Sublette didn't care much for Jimmy's reputation so he stalled him by telling him he only hired veterans. Jimmy was 19 years old, underweight and under-educated, but the Army took him and shipped him at once to France to help drive the Kaiser back. He sniffed mustard gas on his first day in the trenches and they shipped him right back to Arizona.

He was now a veteran. Sublette put him on the Government payroll, but gave him jobs that would keep him out in the country and away from bars.

Jimmy had been many years a patrolman when he rode in from a long week of chasing burros and stray cows back across the Line to the Camou Bros. ranch where they belonged, thus avoiding the onerous chore of writing a seizure report. He stripped the saddle from his tired mount and stumbled around a partition in the Patrol's stable to confront a rat as big as a wildcat and a lot nastier-looking. This rat sat on a bale of hay and was about eye-high to Gleason. He was a gray monster with white whiskers, bits of straw hanging from his shaggy fur, and an insolent sneer.

Jimmy may have been low man on the totem pole around the Patrol but this was too much. He dropped the saddle, drew his Sheriff's Model Colt .45 and in the same motion, fired. The rat jumped, the bullet passed beneath him and through the wall of a stall where aged Captain Sublette's aged white mule was standing hip-shot and asleep and bored right into that beloved animal's stout heart.

Sympathetic fellow officers rushed Jimmy out of the captain's way, but they knew it was only a temporary respite: Jimmy's past with the Patrol may have been long but his future in it would be short.

Shortly after the funeral a contrite Jimmy Gleason rode his horse into the Concordia, reputedly the last man ever to do so, and for that bit of horseplay Collector Leap Cornell, the BIG boss, lifted Jimmy out of the saddle and put him afoot as a Gate inspector. Captain Sublette was gleeful, for that was a duty no self-respecting Mounted Patrolman would have asked for under any circumstances.

But Gleason was a good soldier and did what he was ordered to do. One morning he was unhappily working the Morley Avenue Gate when an angry dog showed up, made threatening gestures with his teeth, slobbered hungrily and growled some surly insults at the inspectors. Two of them ran into the garita, slamming the heavy door on Jimmy Gleason and the mad dog. The dog sprang at Gleason who flaked out his trusted Sheriff's Model and launched a .45 calibre slug at the canine's ugly drooling mouth.

The sound of that shot roared north between the walls of Morley's storefronts, the dog howled and ran across the border with a hole in one ear, the bullet ricocheted off the concrete of International Avenue, sang across Morley, and smashed the transom over the door of the First International Bank, showering glass on the heads of a halfdozen people awaiting its opening.

When a cascade of letters about the indiscriminate discharge of a revolver on crowed downtown streets fell upon the Collector, Cornell put Gleason to work replying to letters from irate

townspeople, the mayor, and as the noise of that shot reached clear to Washington, from congressmen, senators and even the Vice-president.

After Jimmy, poor reader, worse writer, sweated his way through them all, he went back to the Line, swearing to the Collector he would never draw his weapon again.

Maybe not even in self-defense.

The Bumbling Bandit

Jimmy Gleason's hopes of a return to the Patrol were blasted away when the Commissioner of Customs decided the Customs Patrol was not cost effective and discontinued it, thereby opening the borders to a flood of contraband and making a major contribution to the drug problems the U.S. finds itself in today.

Patrolmen suddenly out of a job were blanketed into the Collector's Outside Force as Gate Inspectors. Gleason was one of those. It was either that or quit, and although he was aging he wasn't ready to retire.

The lean little ex-wrapleg, ex-cowboy, ex-patrolman was working the Grand Avenue Gate one evening around six. The sidewalks were full of shopgirls hurrying south to a home in Mexico, and with tourists laden with curios trotting north to catch the 6:30 bus to Tucson. Folks were massed around the door of the bus depot while in Espinosa's money exchange next to it pretty Lupita Amado was readying the cash preparatory to shoving it into the aged safe and closing the shop when a last customer scurried in. *La situacion hace el ladron.*

He was a pale, small, sallow man whose clothes looked big for his scrawny body. He carried a paper shopping bag and now dragged a gun from it that to Lupita had a bore so big and round it looked like Carlsbad Cavern and she expected bats to fly out of it any instant. That a dirty sock was caught on the front sight made no difference. She promptly fainted.

Everything that could go wrong for a bandit began to do so. He dropped the gun in favor of stuffing the cash into the bag that got so heavy the handles broke and money fluttered to the floor. Trying to scoop it and the gun up at the same time, he was surprised by a policeman who walked in and was as surprised as he was. He forgot Lupita, forgot the money, picked up the gun and snapped off a roaring shot at the cop that missed him but knocked a hole out of the storefront window. He headed himself toward Mexico in a dead run in order to escape going back to the prison he had just been let out of.

Folks sort of melted away in front of him and his blazing gun like the waters of the Red Sea parting for Moses and the kids, leaving a clear path to Mexico for this wild-eyed *bandido* firing indiscriminately without care or caution.

Jimmy Gleason was not a highly educated gentleman but would say of himself, "Maybe I can't write and read as good as some of them college boys on the Line, but how many of them could ride into

the hills, read the sign, and come out with a smuggler on the point of his *pistola?*"

Being undereducated did not mean he was stupid. When he saw the man with fixed crazy grin bearing down wildly on his position with a gun that spat real bullets he headed straight for the shelter of the garita, only to find its door blocked by the bodies of fellow officers with a strong instinct for self-preservation.

The delay let his mind catch up with his feet and as he said later, "Here I've been carrying this gun all these years, pounding staples back into fence posts with it, shooting rattlesnakes and coyotes, what am I doing running from somebody that's actually trying to kill me?"

So in spite of his recent misadventures involving firearms, he turned around and fired back just as the robber dashed behind one of the tufa columns that flanked the pedestrian lane into Mexico and the bullet sang off the rock instead of burying itself in the skinny bandit's body.

Across the border a policeman directing traffic saw Gleason shoot, saw the bandit race careening into and through the crowd in front of the Mexican garita waving his revolver. He unlimbered his own. The bumbling bandit ran right into a chunk of .45 calibre lead that decommissioned him instantly.

The policeman's co-workers saw to it that the awkward robber's gun had a couple of full loads in the cylinder instead of all those empties he had been snapping the hammer on, and the policeman didn't even have to face an Inquiry.

Jimmy Gleason did not get off so easily. He was once again forced to compose lengthy letters in his own words to the Bureau of Customs in Washington explaining why he had drawn and fired his piece, even if he did not actually shoot anyone. Not only that, there was an embarrassing investigation that dragged on over six months before he was completely off the hook.

Once more he made the firm resolution never, under any circumstance, to draw his gun again even though there would be times when he was strongly tempted to bend the barrel over the heads of one or two of his over-educated co-workers.

Macho Man

By 12:30 in the morning the day had already started badly for G. Peter, the Immigration Inspector, that ex-cowboy Customs Inspector Jimmy Gleason referred to as the over-educated moron. He was awakened by a taste of ashes in his mouth.

As he suffered from a severe case of hypochondria, he was alarmed by the flavor and rolled out of bed, groaning, to shuffle into the bathroom.

When he turned on the light over the mirror, a colorless bald man peered at him out of red eyes that seemed to be floating on top of violet bags that drooped almost to the end of his long nose.

He opened his mouth to its widest and stuck out his tongue to try to determine what had deposited that odd taste in it. He nearly went into shock at the sight of a strange-looking red growth descending from the roof of his mouth to partially obscure the dark cavern of his throat.

Stifling a frightened scream he hurried into the bedroom to dial the doctor he had hastened to become friendly with on his arrival in Nogales. Lois stirred, opened her eyes, muttered, "What the hell?"

He jabbed a shaking finger at his open mouth. She sat up in alarm. The doctor came on the line and G. Peter said thickly, "Thank god you are home. I just found this thing hanging down in the back of my mouth. Tell me it isn't malignant."

The doctor was not so friendly. "I just got to sleep after delivering two babies and sewing up an accident victim, and you wake me up for that?"

"Isn't it an emergency? I've never seen it before."

"I see it every time I put a tongue depressor in a mouth. It is called the uvula. Take a shot of bourbon, crawl back into bed, and I'll send you my bill in the morning."

By the time G. Peter got settled, Lois was fully awake. She got up and went into the bathroom where she stood looking at herself in the mirror.

No wonder there had been no sex for six months, she thought. In the daytime she could conceal a lot under a blonde wig, heavy eye shadow, tent-like flowing flowered dresses, but whenever she removed her false hair and eyelashes and washed her face, took off her brassiere and her body stocking, everything sagged toward the floor.

It was hard to accept the fact that although she had once been beautiful, it was not easy to find signs of it now. Still, in her worried mind she had room for some fantasies that involved sex with Jaime Hernandez, a suave young neighbor who lived with his mother, and

spent most of his time up at the Hilltop Art Gallery teaching ladies how to paint flowers in oils. He was cordial, paid Lois extravagant compliments on her youthful charm and taste in clothing that a woman fast losing those things under cellulite and wrinkles would be reluctant to disbelieve.

So this day began poorly for both Lois and G. Peter. His troubles didn't stop with his newly-discovered uvula. In the morning, carrying his lunch bucket, he exited home and stepped immediately into a toy wayon left on their porch by some visiting neighborhood kid.

He slid down the steps on his coccyx and his lunch flew all over their lawn. Then he found that the battery on his VW bug had died in the night and when he tried to jump start it from Lois's car he ran that battery down, too.

Forced to hitch-hike to work, on the Line he had to listen as an irate co-worker expressed indignation at such a tardy relief. When G. Peter learned that he would have to work eight hours with Jimmy Gleason whom he detested, for he considered Gleason not only an intellectual zero but retarded as well, it was almost too much.

But that wasn't all. It began to cloud over, thunder roared, rain blew in under the canopy over the traffic lanes to add to G. Peter's misery. When Lois called to tell him the man had come to pump out their septic tank, but had to leave halfway through because his honey-wagon was full, had left the cover off the septic tank and now was going to charge them extra for pumping it out a second time, he nearly came apart.

So when that night Lois, trying vainly to rouse a spark of manhood in him, commented that she wished he was more like Jaime next door, implied they had already had relations and they were out of this world, that did it for G. Peter.

He roared up out of bed hunting for his .38 and Lois, realizing she had unleashed a tiger, called police who rounded G. Peter up before he could get to Jaime.

They put him into one of the city's two jail cells until he could be straightened out, which meant an immediate transfer to Los Angeles where his idiosyncracies would not be so noticeable, taking a contrite and loving Lois with him who by then had nicknamed him her Macho Man.

As for Jaime, G. Peter need never have worried about him. After his mother passed away, he moved to San Francisco and came out of the closet.

The Hero of Morley Avenue

The lookout notice was important enough that the Chief Inspector stayed up late to drop it off at the Gates for the graveyard shifts. Jimmy Gleason and G. Peter were covering Morley Aveune.

The notice had been written by the Customs Agent in Charge and it read:

"Arnold Rossman of Animas, New Mexico, saloonkeeper, will cross this border between midnight and eight this date. He is driving a 1952 Chevrolet pickup and towing a 15-foot boat. He is bringing two brand new gasoline drums each containing 55 gallons of Bacardi rum. Detain and call an agent."

The Chief said, "Whatever else you do tonight, don't let this one through because the CAIC will be over us like an atomic dust cloud only twice as lethal if we let this one get by us."

G. Peter said, "A 15-footer? Why, I had one when I worked —"

The Chief left abruptly. Jimmy walked out to work the small amount of traffic and left G. Peter wagging his tongue that got plenty of exercise for G. Peter could talk on any subject, because according to him he knew something about everything.

The Concordia was unusually quiet, and Jimmy stood in the cool border night listening to the early morning sounds of Nogales, Sonora while Nogales, Arizona slept quietly at his back. There was a scent of boiling coffee drifting across the border on a little breeze up from the south. A cowboy, *muy contento*, came out of the Concordia and wandered south along Elias Street, breaking into song when he was opposite the Caverna and could faintly hear the mariachi music from within.

After his noise faded away, Gleason heard another: a familiar one of a rock bouncing along the pavement of International Avenue, tossed ahead of him by a retarded man aptly called Bulla. If he had a name, nobody knew it.

Bulla's home was the street. It was his nightly custom to select a round rock from the hill behind the graveyard at the west end of International and walk all the way to the Concordia on the east, tossing the rock before him.

Jimmy Gleason walked over to stand beside one of the tufa columns beside the incoming traffic lane, and Bulla, a dark shuffling shadow, came to join him silently, for Bulla could not speak but only made loud and unmelodious sounds, which had earned him the simple nickname, meaning "noise."

But Bulla could communicate non-verbally. He held out his hand and Jimmy dropped a half-dollar into it. Bulla walked across the

street and vanished behind the swinging doors of the Concordia.

Jimmy Gleason returned to the garita where he sat on the cold cement steps with his back to the wall and fought to keep his eyes open until a little after two when all traffic had stopped and he knew there would be no more until about four.

He hurled open the heavy sliding metal door of the garita and yelled, "Get up off that stool and get out here and relieve me, you over-educated ape."

G. Peter awoke with a start, excusing his drowsiness with a muttered speech that went something like: "I, being a *homo sapiens* like yourself have a tendency toward exhaustion at this hour of the day when the human metabolism is lowest and requires large quantities of revitalizing sleep from which I deeply resent being awakened in such a rude and unceremonious manner."

"So take it outside," Jimmy said, "and let me get my share of the shut-eye."

A little past four Jimmy awakened with a vague sense of something not quite right. G. Peter was standing beside him. On his face was the look of one who has just been told that his wife ran off with another man, his house just burned down, his car was stolen, and that both insurance policies had been allowed to lapse. In his hand was the lookout notice.

"Oh, no," Jimmy groaned.

"Nicest man I ever met," G. Peter said defensively. "Pulling this boat and we got into a discussion of its capabilities, I having once owned one like it —"

"Were there two 55-gallon drums in it?"

"He was leaning his elbow on one while we talked."

"How long ago?"

"Two-three minutes. Maybe if I catch him, bring him back, nobody would have to know."

Seeing himself suddenly as the hero saving a bleak situation, correcting his error before it was discovered, G. Peter slammed back the door and dashed out and jumped into his VW and went roaring north on empty Morley Avenue, forgetting to turn on the headlights.

He was building up speed in the long block between the border and East Street, intent on keeping two red taillights in sight, when a pickup pulled out of East and crossed his hurtling path. Swerving sharply to cut in behind it, G. Peter did not see that the pickup had another car in tow on a 30-foot chain.

The Combat Zone

A few Border Inspectors were, and probably are today, allergic to each other. Those who prepare work schedules probably still get their sadistic kicks out of teaming such Inspectors together occasionally in spite of the threat to the peace and harmony in the work place.

The Chief Inspector of Customs at Nogales was one of those, as was the Officer in Charge of the Plant Quarantine Division and the Assistant Officer in Charge of the Immigration and Naturalization Service. To put a little life into the dullness of Gate work they conspired to set up a two-week tour of duty that included Harvey Henderson, the Aggie Inspector, G. Peter, the Immigration Inspector, and Jimmy Gleason, Customs gift to the Arizona Border Services, and sat back to await results.

Mr. Henderson was as lean-faced and gray as his Plant Quarantine Inspector's uniform. His mouth turned down at the corners, pulling vertical grooves into his cheeks. His major contribution to border inspection was an acorn cracker, a wooden device that would crack several acorn shells at once rather than one at a time so that hungry inspectors who had confiscated a handful from border crossers on the pretext of looking for dangerous hitch-hiking bugs could reduce the effort required to crack them one at a time between their teeth.

As a graduate of the University of Oklahoma he had learned a lot about lepidoptera but nothing about the Spanish language. His: "*Lleva frutas o plantas*?" was so Sooner-accented no Mexican could understand him.

Bald-headed G. Peter's conversational bowl over-flowed with long English words and technical phrases learned after two years as a graduate student at Occidental College and he spoke a little Greek, but "*Donde nació*?" was the extent of his knowledge of Spanish.

Customs had no educational requirements beyond a high school education and even that did not apply to men like bowlegged Jimmy Gleason, ex-cowboy blanketed into that Service when the Customs Patrol was abolished.

One thing that Henderson and G. Peter could agree on was that Jimmy Gleason was an absolutely shocking example of the kind of individual who should never have been given a job working with educated people. G. Peter never would forgive Gleason for preventing him from passing an illegal alien through as an American citizen when the man replied: "Michoacan" to his "Donde nació?"

"Not Michigan," Gleason hooted gleefully. "You dumb college graduate, he just said he was born in Michoacan, and that's a State in Mexico."

"No plantas, no frutas, you say," Mr. Henderson once asked indignantly of a lady pedestrian at the Morley Avenue Gate who clutched a sack of groceries to her chest, "this feels like a grapefruit to me!"

She spat out a torrent of Spanish to him.

" 'Hell. no,' she says," Gleason translated between whoops of laughter. "You over-educated idiot, you've got hold of one of her *chi-chis.*"

As a consequence of their antipathy for each other, when border-crossers arrived at the Gate they were forced to make three stops. The inspectional pecking order was Immigration, then Customs, then Agriculture. Most other Inspectors would stand together and ask their specific question of arrivals for a one-stop interrogation, but not this trio.

G. Peter chose to station himself so far south he was nearly in Mexico, Henderson stood so far north he was almost off the 60-foot International Strip, and that left Jimmy Gleason drifting somewhere between them.

It was G. Peter's annoying practice to stop a car, ask his "Where were you born?" then wave the car on as though that constituted the border examination. When that happened to people unaccustomed to border procedures, thinking they were through they would go barrelling down on little Jimmy Gleason who, to stop them, would practically throw his scrawny little body in front of them. Finished with his "What are you bringing from Mexico?" routine he would wave them on and they would roar past Henderson, who would pound their fenders and race after them shouting: "Halt! Halt! Any fruit or plants?"

Many letters of complaint were written about this strange procedure but nothing would bring these three closer together except cold weather.

It was such a night when an arctic wind damp with rain and sleet drove them into the only shelter available, the small Morley Avenue garita. To make matters worse for G. Peter and Henderson, Jimmy started a rambling yarn about his knock-down-and-drag-out battles in the Concordia, that saloon just a few steps into Mexico from the garita where even then they could hear sounds of violent confrontation.

Gleason was just getting to the climax of his story when out of Mexico stumbled a wild-eyed man dodging, weaving, and punching at shadows. He stopped in front of the garita and yelled at the men inside, "Come out and fight, you ugly sons of bitches."

G. Peter and Henderson promptly roared out the door. After a strenuous five minutes they threw the combative inebriate back

across the Line. Much disheveled and out of breath they tramped into the garita to find Jimmy Gleason placidly looking at the *Nogales Daily Herald.*

Their bitter indignation spilled over into: "You were bragging on your prowess as a saloon battler, why weren't you out there helping us?"

"Because," Gleason replied, "you highly-qualified morons, he wasn't talking to me."

Buried in Concrete

The Morley Avenue garita had been designed by someone who had never been west of the Potomac, but who had read somewhere that there were occasional violent revolutions in Mexico that sometimes spilled over into the United States. Consequently the garita was built more with the thought of providing shelter from flying bullets than of comfort for Inspectors on duty.

It was — and still is — a solid blockhouse with concrete walls 16 inches thick. A rear window and two side windows were as narrow as gunslots. In the glass of these and the windows in the metal sliding doors was embedded a kind of chicken wire to make them shatterproof in the event lead began to zip wildly into the United States from Mexico as it had from time to time in the past. The front window, facing the lane, was of single strength glass. A wooden canopy extended out over the lane, providing some shelter for Inspectors from sun, and from rain falling straight down.

A feature made necessary by the prevalence of smugglers bringing booze out of Mexico during Prohibition, was heavy mirrors built on a slant into the edge of a concrete platform raised eight inches above the floor of the lane. In the lane's floor were sunken lights protected by strong iron mesh. On one of the two columns supporting the end of the canopy away from the garita was a light switch. By activating the lights and glancing down into the mirrors, an Inspector standing on the raised platform could view the entire underside of a vehicle without having to kneel and get his hands and knees dirty.

Even after repeal, Inspectors insisted that the custodial help daily clean the lights on the lane floor and the mirrors and if they failed to do it, often did it themsleves, for although they seldom looked under cars anymore the lights and mirrors still served a purpose.

It is hard to pinpoint exactly who made the initial discovery because people have a tendency to keep a good thing to themselves, but it is generally assumed that it was Al Martin, an Immigration Inspector, who accidentally released the secret.

Martin was a large man whose uniforms fitted him as tightly as though he had grown into them, especially around the stomach. He had sparse blonde hair, thick lips, a red face, and wore dark glasses even at night with the visor of his six-pointed cap tugged down over his eyes like Moammar Khadafy.

He was working slow car and pedestrian traffic alone one cold night, standing on that platform, while the other Inspectors awaited their time in the barrel in the warm garita. Martin was hunkered into his overcoat as far as its restrictions would permit, longing for a hot

toddy, a steaming cup of coffee, anything in the way of a stimulant.

In answer to his desires, here it came in the person of an attractive young lady carrying a reed-wrapped jug of Bacardi rum out of Mexico, walking into the dimly-lit lane, staggering just a little.

Martin reached out and turned on the lights in the floor of the lane. "Come over here, young lady," he said, "and declare your citizenship and what you have there."

She complied pleasantly, they had a little more conversation, during which she innocently and automatically lifted one foot to put it on the platform.

The Inspectors inside saw Martin's interest and, wondering at it, hurriedly emerged from the garita to join him, lining up on the platform like rapacious buzzards, hunched inside their greatcoats, glances downcast like his was. And from then on, whenever opportunity presented itself, Inspectors were able to indulge in a form of surreptitious Peeping Tommery.

Eventually, of course, all good things do come to an end, and the Morley Avenue amusement arcade was closed down.

It happened this way: Al Martin again, interrogating a young woman, flanked by two assisting Inspectors. The lady, the secretary of a Congressman, was not stupid and read their interest in her correctly, especially when she had glanced down to determine the cause of their intent downward gazes.

Her complaint about being visually gang-raped by a bunch of uncouth border Inspectors was heeded. Today, the result of her complaint can still be seen at Morley Avenue, a monument to one woman's virtue.

The mirrors and lights are solidly buried in concrete.

Showdown at Sulphur Springs

(This chapter orignally appeared in AMERICAN WEST magazine for June 1988. Used with permission.)

Lieutenant Britton Davis — a handsome, well-groomed, soft-spoken Texan and graduate of West Point — was an unlikely partner in a conspiracy to defraud the United States government out of customs duties due.

His partner was the Apache Geronimo, a violent, treacherous terrorist with a long record of leading raids against settlers both north and south of the Mexican border. Early in 1884, while in Sonora, Mexico, Geronimo agreed to stop plundering and take his band of Chiricahua Apaches back to the San Carlos Apache Reservation in Arizona Territory.

At the time, the commander of U.S. Army forces in the Department of Arizona was General George Crook, famous as a relentless Indian fighter. Crook sent Davis, with scouts and mule packers, to meet Geronimo at the Mexican border near the old San Bernardino Ranch in the southeast corner of Arizona Territory.

The lieutenant was under orders to escort the renegade and his company, which included a herd of stolen Mexican cattle, to the San Carlos Reservation, about 175 miles to the northwest. Davis's mission was to protect the nearly one hundred Indians from the well-deserved wrath of irate citizens of the Territory as the caravan made its way up the Sulphur Springs Valley and along the Gila River to the Reservation. With his unit of Apache scouts for support, the lieutenant was to prevent the Indians from breaking off and committing further depredations.

Davis faced immediate problems. He had not counted on some "350 head of beeves, cows, and half-grown calves" which could make only twenty miles per day at best. He had planned to travel twice as fast in an effort to avoid contact with American or Mexican settlers. He also hadn't counted on Geronimo's constant demands to stop and let the animals rest and feed. Geronimo did not make Davis's job easy, for the Apache's natural mood was foul. When anything displeased him, and everything on the march did, he threatened to turn around and go back to Mexico, murdering and pillaging as he went.

They were already behind schedule when the caravan reached the Sulphur Springs Ranch, thirty miles west of Fort Bowie. Here Geronimo put down his deerskin boot and refused to go farther until his cattle and horses were fed, watered, and rested. He wanted, he said emphatically, to reach the Reservation with fat stock that would command a high price, not four-legged skeletons he would take a loss on. Geronimo demanded three days of rest for his animals. Davis gave him one day.

The ranch house was an adobe structure surrounded by a five-foot wall of the same material enclosing a couple of acres. The pack train went into camp fifty yards from the house, while Davis's Apache scouts camped a little farther out. Since a chill breeze was blowing, several hostile families, including Geronimo's, settled in the lee of the wall. Others scattered around nearby waterholes, and the livestock, bunched by Apache herders, grazed a half-mile away.

Davis had just pitched his tent when two men came out of the ranch house and approached him. They introduced themselves as federal officers, one as the United States Marshal for Southern Arizona, the other as a representative of the United States Collector of Customs. The federal agents told Davis that the cattle were contraband smuggled into the country from Mexico, and ordered him to help them seize Geronimo's livestock because no customs duty had been paid. They demanded that he assist in arresting the Apache leader for the murder of a number of Arizona settlers.

The agents had the mild-mannered lieutenant in a box. If he and his scouts attempted to grab Geronimo, the Apache's reaction would be swift and bloodthirsty. If Davis survived that, he would probably be kicked out of the army. And if Arizonans did not hang him from a limb of the nearest tree for letting Geronimo escape, the federal court and jail lurked in the background.

Then out of the darkening east rode salvation in the saddle bags of an Old West Point chum, Lieutenant John "Bo" Blake, stationed at Fort Boise. Having known in advance that Davis would be at the ranch, Blake came to visit, bringing along a full bottle of scotch whiskey. Putting off any decisive action until morning, Davis invited the two federal agents to join him and Blake in consuming the scotch, which the army officers poured generously for their guests.

When the bottle was empty, the marshal and the customs collector staggered off to their bedrolls on the ranch house porch. Davis and Blake sat and talked until they heard snores from the house. Then Davis sent for Geronimo, who was most unhappy at being awakened in the middle of the night. The mean-tempered Apache would have none of Davis's plan until something about it presented a challenge and appealed to his crafty sense of humor.

After Geronimo left with Blake, Davis sat down outside the ranch house to wait for dawn. The sun was well over the horizon before anyone stirred on the porch. The first man out of his bed was the customs collector, and it wasn't long before he realized that something was wrong. "They're gone!" he bellowed, "they're gone!"

When the lawmen calmed down, Davis pointed out that the Apaches had a ten-hour start. By the time they could be overtaken, they would be on the San Carlos Reservation with the cattle scattered and Geronimo in hiding. Davis did not have to detail how their situation might be seen by their superiors in Washington: two trusted government employees got drunk and slept through a mass exodus of 96 Apaches, 33 Indian scouts, 11 packers, a herd of cattle, 77 horses, and 15 saddled mules — all under the command of Lieutenant Bo Blake.

The federal agents rode sadly away with their hangovers.

The saga did not end so happily for Geronimo as it did for Davis. The Apache's livestock was taken away and later sold for $1,762.50, which was distributed to the Mexicans from whom the animals had been stolen.

End of an Era

Billy Cardwell left San Diego on the day after the new sound of generators from searchlights on the hill behind his rented Encanto house probing the sky for Japanese aircraft kept him awake all night.

He drove a straight 18 hours at 35 miles an hour into Arizona and arrived at the border in time to report for Customs duty with another recruit named Leslie Wisdom, who had just arrived from Missouri. Neither of them was shaved or showered.

On that day Chief Inspector Randolph Adams lifted his iron-rimmed eyeglasses off one big purple ear at a time and stepped off the box he stood on so he could see over the counter he was behind. He was five-feet-five, so skinny his bones rattled, and his lined face wore the sad look of a barefoot man who has just stepped into a pile of fresh dog do.

He spread thin arms in gartered sleeves along the high counter, put the sharp point of his veined nose five inches above their papers and lip-read them in a whisper. His mouth moved like he was nibbling an ear of moldy Indian corn. With his head wobbling on the end of his wrinkled neck tucked down between sharp shoulders hunched, he looked like an aging buzzard minutely inspecting carrion and not particularly impressed by what he saw.

But neither diminished stature nor the scavenger-like appearance he presented lessened his air of authority. Chief Inspector Adams was never called Randy by anybody. Even his wife called him *Mister* Adams.

He talked terrier, biting the tail off each word. "Cardwell?" he snapped.

"I'm the tall one, Chief Adams, sir."

"Commercial artist, it says here. Music writer. Six feet tall." He sniffed. "Shouldn't you be in uniform?"

"I will be," Cardwell said, deliberately misinterpreting, "a Customs Inspector's, as soon as I can get one."

He wanted to add that he would also go to war if he had to, not because he wanted to, but this did not seem the appropriate time to say so.

Chief Adams sniffed again as if nasally tracking an elusive stink bomb. "All of us here on the border are veterans of one war or another. Women paint pictures here in Nogales, and write music for church services and the like." His scalp was dry and grey through sparse white hair. "San Diego. Married." He looked up quickly. "Wife here?"

CSP

"Not yet."

"Then don't go disgracing the uniform you haven't even got yet, chasing women up and down Canal Street." He shuffled Cardwell's papers aside. "Mr. Wisdom?"

The other wartime recruit Customs border guard said, "Yo."

Chief Adams looked up sharply. His eyes were pale sky over the North Pole.

"Present," Wisdom corrected swiftly. Adams sniffed.

Wisdom was as short as he was wide. And round. Red round face, little round brown eyes. Small mouth with one corner turned up, one down.

Chief Adams read and sniffed some more. "St. Louis. Married. One child, your wife here?"

"No."

"Same advice to you." Adams lip-read some more. "Car salesman. Used?"

"New. Only there aren't any around any more."

"Making bullets out of the metal to kill the Japs with," Chief Adams snapped, looking at Cardwell accusingly. He returned his glasses to their rightful place, one ear at a time, settled them on the wedge of his nose with both hands, swept their papers into a pile, transferred the pile to a spur-scarred wooden desk, Pancho Villa period, behind him.

He brought from beneath the countertop two heavy .38 calibre Colt Special Police revolvers, the one on the .45 frame. Beside them he laid two thin black books with the title in gold letters: MANUAL FOR THE GUIDANCE OF THE COLLECTOR'S OUTSIDE FORCE. A couple of badges and cap insignias.

"That's your equipment. Sign here. Lose it, pay for it. You're the Collector's Outside Force now, and outside is where you'll work, rain or snow, sleet, wind, or sun. Any questions?" He didn't sound like he was encouraging any and frowned when Wisdom raised his hand tentatively.

"Yes, Mr. Wisdom?"

"Where's the men's room, Randy?"

It was the end of one era, the beginning of another.

The Tea Party

The first rains come to the border country in mid-summer and from the first fallen drops the tan-colored hills and deserts begin to green. Much of the cool color comes from *quelites de las aguas* and whole families take to the hills to harvest the young and tender leaves.

When they are about as high as a hand held horizontally on edge along the ground, quelites are at their best. They can be cooked like spinach, fried, or eaten raw, as in salads.

Aging quickly in desert heat, they turn tough, bristly, and inedible. A straight stalk emerges from the plant like a rocket and heads for the blue sky, then bends double and shakes loose hundreds of thousands of grains of pollen per plant.

The eyes of many people begin to wink, blink, itch, they sniffle, sneeze, and wheeze, throats grow sore, voices drop into the bass clef, more water springs from tortured nostrils than flows down the desert's dry washes in the rainy season.

Billy Cardwell was one of those who suffered all the symptoms, the red runny nose, wheezes, red-rimmed eyes. These did not fit his picture of a macho Border Customs Inspector, wearing a Colt .38 holstered low on his thigh, the strap of a blackjack hanging from his hip pocket and a set of handcuffs dangling from his belt at the small of his back, so he tried to keep it under control so no one would notice.

He tried all the remedies and settled on one to help his breathing. It was a powdered mixture of dried herbs containing belladonna and Cardwell suspected, from its distinctive odor when burning, Indian hemp. When ignited and the smoke was inhaled, this remedy dramatically alleviated, temporarily, Cardwell's breathing troubles. Eye drops and nasal sprays took care of the rest, but for the most part the season of the maturing quelites was a miserable one for him.

Once during this period he was paired with big, rough Joe Beck whom he quickly grew to admire, a man who seemed never to have had a sick day in his life, or if he had, nobody was ever allowed to know about it.

On their first midnight shift together Joe came into the garita lugging a huge cardboard Kotex box under his arm. He set it on the counter and unloaded.

It was like he had planned a long weekend away from home. Out of that box came large supplies of food and drink, a half-dozen books, a sweater, a carton of Camel cigarettes, two vacuum bottles, one filled with coffee, one with milk; a radio for listening to the early morning talk shows, the newspaper from the day just passed, and sundry homey items to make himself comfortable, including a pair of slippers for big feet.

Shortly after two, traffic dropped dramatically. Joe went into the garita and laid out his sumptuous lunch of cream cheese, bread, butter, soup, Vienna sausage, salad in a paper cup, two fried chicken legs, cheese cake, and coffee.

The Aggie Inspector had gone home at midnight on his Department's assumption that no dangerous insects would cross the border in contaminated fruit until eight in the morning. That left Billy Cardwell alone to work the car lane and any pedestrians that chanced to pass before five when the local crosser-workers would start to file over from Sonora.

A breeze sprang up, blowing gently east, out of Holler Canyon that was choked with the noxious pigweed the tender quelites had become, swept down dusty International Avenue, and up Billy Cardwell's nostrils. He began to choke up and sneeze, and he stuffed Kleenex up his nose to stop the flow of water so Joe Beck would not suspect his disgraceful weakness.

As soon as Joe finished his lunch he came out to take his turn in the barrel. Billy hurried gasping into the garita, dug his can of pulverized weeds out of his lunch bucket and dashed into the tiny toilet room where he took some of the material out of the can, put it in the lid, put a match to it and inhaled the smoke. He opened the little window a bit to let out the strong odor of burned grass he couldn't smell but knew would linger.

Relief came quickly. In minutes he came out to the counter and ate his meager meal of beef tea and a piece of jerky, for food only stuffed him up and made it harder for him to breathe. In a little while here came Joe Beck, with a customer with a re-entry permit, so Cardwell had to go out into the heavey pollen again and run the shop until Joe was through. When in a bit the border crosser emerged, got into his car and drove north, Joe went back to the toilet. Seconds later he loped out, eyes big, saying, "Billy, call the Agents."

Cardwell said, "Whatever for?"

"I let that man use the toilet and he had a tea party."

"How do you know?"

"You can smell grass."

"He wasn't in there long enough to toke up."

"You don't call," Joe said, "I will."

Cardwell couldn't quite see confessing his weakness to an irate Customs Agent awakened from sleep to follow an elusive trail of non-existent marijuana. He confessed.

Joe Beck never mentioned Cardwell's problem to anyone. A secret one of his own made him compassionate. Something Cardwell had not known until then was that in the Kotex box Joe Beck carried his personal artillery kit. He was shooting up, on the needle, a great big monkey on his back he would never shake, and in the end it would carry him off, for Joe Beck had diabetes.

Suffer the Little Children

Joe Beck was the kind of man you liked to have on shift with you because he was big, gruff, rough and tough. He was on duty at the Grand Avenue Gate in Nogales when a man in his forties drove out of Mexico with his two young sons.

As he had bought merchandise to follow, he had to go into the garita to make out a declaration, those being the times when you could declare merchandise to follow and bring it in duty-free under your exemption.

The boys came and stood by Joe on the concrete base of the garita to wait for their father to come out. They both wore bib overalls and were barefooted and sunburned.

Joe said, "Where you been, boys?"

The older one had red hair. "Over at the ocean," he said, "We caught a shark this big." He showed Joe with his hands.

"What'd you catch him on?"

"Bait," the younger boy said. "Meat out of the head of a dorado."

Then he looked at his feet and crowded closer to his brother, who put an arm around his thin shoulders and messed his blonde hair gently. Their backs were to the doorway into the garita where their father was talking with the Shift Captain.

"What's your name?" Joe asked the older boy.

"Sammy Williams."

"Yours?"

The little fellow said, "Jim Boy."

"Williams," prompted his brother.

Inside the garita, the boys' father fell over backward. All Joe could see of him was his legs and feet. The feet were drumming on the hard concrete floor of the garita. The Shift Captain stood paralyzed, staring down at him. The boys had not seen.

Joe Beck said, "You boys know what epilepsy is?"

Sammy said, "What is it?"

"Fits. Your daddy ever have them?"

"Naw," Sammy said with a half grin that faded altogether as he turned, saw his father down.

He ran inside. Jim Boy, bewildered, followed him.

Joe Beck strode into the garita. The Shift Captain was on his knees, loosening Williams shirt. Beck went to the phone and called for oxygen and an ambulance. He had hardly hung up when the siren opened up from a block away.

Williams was now completely quiet. His eyelids were almost closed.

CSP

Jim Boy looked at Sammy. "Is Daddy asleep?"

Sammy looked at Joe Beck. "He is, sir, isn't he?"

Joe said, "He was very tired, boys."

Amy Guthrie, the only woman mortician on the border, hurried in. She knew at a glance. She shook her head.

Joe Beck put a gentle hand on a shoulder of each of the boys and said, "Fellers, your daddy is pretty sick. This nice lady will take him in the ambulance. Now, Sammy, you're the man of the family. Tell me your momma's name and her telephone number."

"Got no momma." That was Jim Boy answering.

"Grandparents?"

Sammy said, "Grandpa Joe and Grandma Joan. Their telephone is Garfield 4456."

"Where do they live?"

"Los Angeles."

Both boys went to their father as the Shift Captain and Amy put him on a stretcher. Jim boy took his father's limp dangling hand, pressed it to his cheek.

Sammy put his arm around the younger boy's shoulder. "Let them take him," he said.

Jim Boy turned and burrowed his head into Sammy's side just under the armpit. Sammy held him tightly.

Joe Beck got the grandparents on the phone, told them what had happened, let each boy talk to them. Then he took the phone back and said, "Don't worry about them. I'm taking them home with me. I've got two boys of my own. We'll look out for them until you get here."

A few days after the grandparents had come and picked up the boys, Joe Beck got a letter that read:

"The salary of a Government employee doesn't begin to pay for the compassion you and your wife and boys showed our grandchildren. We will never forget your kindness to them. Neither will they, for every time they remember their father, they will remember you. May God always be with you."

Joe Beck never showed that letter to anybody, but when he, too, checked out of this world, it was found among his effects.

The Last Good Game

When Billy Cardwell joined the Collector's Outside Force at Nogales he was 10 years younger than the youngest veteran Customs Inspector. He was eager, ambitious, and ignorant of the unspoken rules of conduct for Inspectors in the Arizona District: see nothing, hear nothing, do nothing, know nothing, don't rock the gravy boat and you last long enough to retire.

Anson Ramsey had broken all those rules and swam upstream against the current which was why he was never popular with his co-workers and one of the reasons why he was Assistant Chief Inspector and none of them were.

He gave Billy the first piece of sage advice: "You've probably been taught that the customer is always right. Forget it, this is one place the customer is always wrong."

Ramsey had reference to border inspections and the standard Customs question: "What are you bringing from Mexico?" For even if the reply was: "Nothing," if an Inspector insisted on looking in a car's trunk to verify the answer and look for undeclared, restricted, or prohibited goods, he was implying that the border-crosser was a liar until proven otherwise.

Anson Ramsey was tall, gaunt, old. His rough toughness granted himself no leeway just because he wore corrective lenses so thick and heavy they had made a permanent dent in the bridge of his nose. His uniform cap was a size 8 and inside his grey unkempt head was a storehouse of miscellaneous Customs lore bigger than that of the best-informed executive in the Bureau of Customs in the District of Columbia.

This treasure trove he had also consigned to the typewritten pages of a black loose-leaf binder he kept in the lower right drawer of the ancient, spur-scarred desk in the office he shared with the Chief. He had in it the answers to all the questions, but nobody ever asked any until Billy Cardwell came to work, wanting to know all there was to know right now, reminding Ramsey of himself when he had entered the Service so long before.

One of Anson's close friends and confidants was Larry Thompson, janitor at the Federal Building. He shared Ramsey's affliction, near-blindness. They both laughed about that, Thompson often saying he was well-qualified to be a Customs Inspector because they never saw anything, anyway.

They shared other things. They both liked good food, good drinks, and good poker. Larry kept a bottle hidden in a trash bin in the basement behind the furnace so they could, somewhere between

four and five p.m., get a start on their pre-dinner drinks before they stopped for the rest of them at the Elks Club and a few hands of poker.

Anson didn't drive any more, so when he had enough of a game and wasn't winning, he would call Faye, who was his eyes (although she was losing sight, too), and she would come and drive Larry to his residence — if he was not riding a good luck streak — and then take Anson to their home on Walnut.

But Anson Ramsey never played poker again after one particularly good game where he was holding all the winning hands. He called Faye to share the news with her and to ask her to come for him.

He got no answer, so he walked home, where he found her dead. Yesterday had been their wedding anniversary. In the excitement of winning he had completely forgotten he had promised to take her to La Caverna for dinner.

Two days after the funeral, Anson Ramsey trudged into the Inspection Room carrying a big pottery piggy bank and walked into his office without a word to Billy Cardwell, who was holding down the railroad desk, filling in for the regular man, who was on vacation.

Billy wanted to express sympathy but Ramsey was such a hard old buzzard he might not welcome it and probably would say something like: "Blow it out your ear," only he would not have said "ear." So Billy sat tight until the office door opened and Ramsey called him in. The office smelled like an old barroom.

There was a pile of odds and ends on the scarred desk and a couple of wastebaskets were overflowing. Ramsey said, "Been going to clean up this rat's nest for a long time." He handed Billy his worn black loose-leaf notebook, thick with the notes he had typed into it. "You can get more out of this than I can. I can't even read it any more. Now drive me over to Madre Conchita's orphanage."

On the way there, Ramsey said, "When Faye got mad at me she would drop coins into a piggy bank, some kind of penance." He sighed. "We made a lot of trips."

Man cleans out his desk, starts giving stuff away, drinks more than usual, nobody should have been surprised. Bourbon and Black Leaf Forty make a powerful draught, a lethal one.

Thirty years later, retiring Billy Cardwell cleaned out his own desk in the Bureau of Customs in Washington. One of the books in his bookcase was Anson Ramsey's worn black notebook, thicker with additions that Cardwell had made down the years. He left it on the shelf. It had been his passport out of the dead end job on the Line. For someone else, Anson Ramsey's lifework—and some of Billy Cardwell's — would provide a lift up the career stairway.

The Little Black Bears

Some folks in Arizona will remember those good days when you could bring $500 worth of merchandise out of Mexico duty-free and include a gallon of booze.

A week after the Cardwells arrived in Nogales, Cardwell came home late from working the evening shift.

"What exciting event detained you?" Maureen asked.

"I had to write up a Section 497 seizure I made just before I was relieved," Cardwell explained.

"What kind of seizure is that? Is it catching?"

"It's a failure to declare, I had to collect the penalty."

"What's the penalty?"

"An amount equal to the domestic value thereof."

"I love it when you talk legal. What's domestic value?"

"In this case the price paid plus duty and internal revenue. It was liquor."

"What happens to the liquor?"

"It's poured down the drain."

"Creating a bunch of inebriated sewer rats? What if it isn't liquor that is not declared?"

"Procedure's the same except that every once in awhile Customs has an auction of goods seized."

"Seems easy. That all?"

"Well, there's the 592. False declaration."

"Clarify, please."

"Say somebody comes from Mexico and says he hasn't brought anything from Mexico in the last 31 days —"

"Why 31 days?"

"Well, the Tariff Act says a person coming from another country can only bring in, free of duty, goods for his own personal use if he hasn't brought any in the last 30 days, —"

"You said 31."

"There has to be 30 days elapse between the day you brought anything the last time and the day you're bringing any this time."

"Let's ease on past this one."

Cardwell said, "The reason this gets complicated is that there are so many ramifications."

"Name one."

"Residents and non-residents are treated differently."

"So where does the false declaration come in?" Her forehead was puckered with thought-wrinkles.

"If you would just let me finish this piece by piece," Cardwell said.

"Suppose the man —"

"What if it's a woman?"

"The law says person. Regardless of age. A man with a family of 14 could bring 14 gallons of liquor. Anyway, this person says he hasn't carried anything out of Mexico in the last 31 days, then we find out he did. That's one example."

"How do you know he lied?"

"Well. there's this card file, see, importations valued under a certain amount, Inspectors write out this card, a short form declaration —"

"What if they don't use the short form procedure?"

Cardwell yawned and Maureen said, "I'm boring you?"

"No," he said. "I'm boring me."

"Go on. I never did know what you do down there except ask where were you born?"

"That's Immigration. Customs says what are you bringing."

"The short form declaration," she prompted.

"As opposed to a long form. Somebody checks it against the file to see if he's brought anything in the last 30 days under Paragraph 1798 —"

"What if he uses another name?"

"False declaration. We ask for ID."

"What if he says he doesn't have any?"

"We wring him out."

"If he's lying?"

"We seize the goods."

"Like the 497?"

"Not exactly. There is a difference."

"Is there anything else I should know about?"

"Well, there's this Paragraph 1798."

"What's with it?"

"It has to do with exemptions folks coming into the United States are entitled to depending on their residence status."

"Does that have anything to do with being a citizen?"

"No."

"And you get into this stuff simply by asking where were you born?"

"What are you bringing?"

"How'd you catch this one?"

"Which one?"

"The one that made you late."

"Well, this man declared two gallons of rum. They were in plain sight. One for him, one for his son, who was playing with a couple of little black bear key chains the makers of Oso Negro gin and vodka put on each bottle as an advertising gimmick. As the liquor in sight was rum, I asked the boy where the bottles the little bears came off of were and he pointed under the seat."

The Trouble at Tres Bellotas

When Mike Rakowski came from Detroit to the border to join the Collector's Outside Force he had no intention of getting married and settling down. He was young, blond, handsome, liked his drinks and girls, was a normal cleancut Polish-American boy in every way and could not quite picture himself in a life of domesticity tied to only one woman.

There was a surplus of girls in the border port and single men revelled in this harvest. Mike was no exception. So when Josefina Arriaga, the most attractive of them all, led him to the altar in Sacred Heart Church where Father Larry Quigley discussed his golf game as he tied the knot, Mike was dazed with the suddeness of it all.

Mike and Fina got along well, even blissfully, as soon as she made him understand he was never even to as much as smile at any of his old girl friends. She kept him on such a tight rein he couldn't even get out with the boys. He gradually got used to being in harness.

A few days before Christmas he was looking forward to proceeding directly home from work and having a couple of tequilitas with Fina in front of the fireplace and a blazing Yule log in their new burnt-adobe home as he wound up a four to midnight shift on the Gate.

Billy Cardwell was the Shift Captain, Charley Evans was the other Customs man on duty, and they were talking about going over to the Concordia for a couple of innocent unwinders. They invited Mike to join them but he politely declined in favor of his tryst with Fina.

Plans were abruptly altered when Tom Wilson, the Customs Agent in Charge, dashed into the garita gasping, "Billy, I need help. Some trucks loaded with goods are going to cross into Mexico over at Tres Bellotas and all my agents are out of town. If we hurry we can intercept them."

As Tres Bellotas was not a port of entry, crossings at that ranch were illegal, be they exportations or importations. There was the possiblity that among the goods might be some that were on the Positive List and prohibited exportation or at the least required licensing.

Cardwell looked at Charley Evans. "I always try to do at least one good turn a day. There'll be nothing in it but lost sleep for us, but what do you say?"

"Anything to help a friend," Evans replied.

So Cardwell and Evans called their wives to let them know they would be late. Mike was torn between his wish to be helpful and his desire to get cozy with Fina and finally said, "Let me check with Fina."

She, too, had been eagerly awaiting this evening with him, but she reluctantly gave him permission to help Wilson and urged him to hurry home afterward. She would wait up for him.

They made their high speed run 30 miles on the Tucson-Nogales highway to Arivaca Junction, drove fast over the dirt road to Arivaca ahead of their funnel of dust, swept south to Oro Blanco and into the rutted Tres Bellotas road. Dust was hanging in the air and they were afraid they had arrived too late until they caught up with their quarry just a quarter-mile short of the International Line.

That was only because a long well-drilling rig had gotten crosswise on the trace that led up a steep hill to the border and was stuck there in such a way no other vehicle could pass. Lined up behind it were six pickups loaded with Christmas toys and goodies.

Philosophically, the drivers had built a roaring campfire, were toasting *tripas de leche* on a grill, one had a guitar, there was singing and laughter and several bottles of tequila passing among them as they waited for dawn's early light so they could see how to surmount their current obstacle.

One of the drivers tossed a bottle to Mike, and some of it sloshed on his uniform when he caught it. He was sorely tempted, but immediately gave it to Charley Evans who upended it gleefully as a proper substitute for the drinks he had been going to have in the comfortable surroundings of the Concordia Club.

Cardwell and Wilson, pondering their next move, came over and squatted on their heels by the fire, absently accepting bottles of tequila every time they went by.

"So now what?" Wilson asked, slyly passing the buck along with a bottle.

Cardwell said, "It being Christmas and all, I would be inclined to let them go if I could be sure they have nothing prohibited aboard because all they are trying to do is bypass their own Customs service."

"Can't do that," Wilson said thoughtfully. "Can we?"

"If we could break that well-rig out we could take them back to Nogales and let the Collector decide what to do."

Mike interjected, "I'm an ex-truck driver. Get the other vehicles out of the way and I'll get it loose."

They cleared a path, Mike jumped into the cab of the well-rig, started the engine, slammed it into reverse and came roaring backward off the hill.

In caravan they made a slow return to the Arivaca Junction where Cardwell suggested they stop at Kinsley's roadhouse for coffee.

Mike was in the lead as they trooped into the restaurant. The lone waitress put down her newspaper and with a yell of delight, launched herself exuberantly at Mike. She was one of his many former playmates.

"Aw, Marta," he said, "all I have time for is a cup of coffee."

It was nearly eight in the crisp December morning before they had their seized vehicles and merchandise lined up in the Customs compound and could go home.

Billy Cardwell was just settling gratefully into sleep when Maureen brought him the telephone on a long cord.

"It's Mike," she said. "He says it's urgent."

There was desperation in Mike's voice. "Billy," he cried, "you gotta help me. I stumbled on the top porch step, Fina was waiting behind the screen door. Then she smelled the tequila I spilled on me, then she saw a smudge of lipstick on my collar that Marta left from her friendly hug, and now she won't let me in!"

When Cardwell called Fina and convinced her it was all circumstantial evidence and Mike was innocent of any wrongdoing he told Maureen he wouldn't have to do another good deed all day, he'd already done two.

That's All for 31 Days

Once upon a time everyone who crossed the Mexican border bringing liquor or goods valued at more than $25 under their duty-free exemption had to make a written declaration. They had to get out of their car, stand at attention, and raise their right hand and swear under oath that their declaration was the truth, the whole truth, and nothing but the truth, and sign it before a United States Customs Inspector.

These declarations were filed and the file daily examined to see that the prohibition against more than one duty-free importation a month had not been violated. At Nogales the Inspector on the graveyard shift arranged them in alphabetical order, a clerk in the headquarters office above the Post Office compared them with the ones on file and weeded out the ones that were older than 30 days.

The volume of traffic crossing the border began to increase, complaints began to pour in about the length of time it took to cross, and the Immigration Inspectors on the graveyard shift found that, under the dual-screening program, they were working half their tour alone doing Customs work while the Customs Inspector sat inside the garita and alphabetically arranged declarations.

This led to the introdution of the oral declaration for the one-gallon quota of alcoholic beverages and less than $25 worth of merchandise. But Inspectors were not released from the obligation to inform declarants that would be all the goods they might bring duty-free for 31 days.

The absurdity of saying: "That will be all you can bring duty-free for 31 days" when there was no way to check whether the regulation had been violated or not was early obvious to Inspectors, whose wives complained that they even repeated the phrase in their sleep.

No official notice of this ridiculousness was taken in Nogales until one day in January of 1946 the Collector received the following letter:

"My dear Sir:

Last night I crossed the border at Nogales. The Inspector was surly and uncommunicative and insisted in looking in the trunk even when I told him there was nothing in it. Then he pawed through my suitcase and did not put it back in its former state of neatness. When I told him I had nothing to declare he kept saying, 'That's all you can bring duty-free for 31 days.'

I have discussed this incident with our University psychologists and the following diagnosis was obtained: Customs Inspectors feel

CJP

very insecure. They have to assert their authority as compensation for their lack of security. They actually resent their work and location and try to overdo the job so the guilt feelings associated with dislike for the work place will be compensated by a seemingly successful discovery of a number of smugglers and other quantitatively expressed achievements. They need constant reassurance. They need a vacation or a transfer from surroundings that have unpleasant associations in their subconscious. They must have rather a hard life financially. The problems of home and daily life, i.e., security of employment, joy of work, need to be ironed out.

Please call on me if you need further assistance. Sincerely,"

The signature on the letter was not legible, but after receiving it, Collector Leap Cornell drove from his office over the Post Office to see if his Inspectors were really in need of psychological help. He came up behind one who was about to conclude his tour after coping with horrendous traffic for eight hours.

Just as the Collector moved in on him, a car plastered with religious bumper stickers, laden with happy, singing people full of Christian zeal, drove up. The tired Inspector asked: "What are you bringing from Mexico?"

In joyful chorus the group replied, "Nothing but Jesus in our hearts, Brother."

The harried Inspector said, "That will be all you can bring duty-free for 31 days," and waved them on.

A False Declaration

At their luncheon meeting on Wednesday in a year before World War II the members of Nogales Rotary International had a surprise speaker. The Program Chairman said, "We have been after Collector of Customs, Leap Cornell, to talk to us for many years. When he called this morning and said he would today it meant postponing our scheduled speaker, but I jumped at the opportunity and here he is."

Applause was tentative, for Cornell was a controversial figure. A grey-haired, hawk-nosed man, he had been a railroader, gambler, banker, rancher, financier and had even worked the other side of the street before becoming Collector.

Lost in the dim past and dusty files was the time he had crossed the border in his Saxon automobile at an unauthorized place with such a heavy load of Waterfill and Frazier that Customs Patrolmen in a Dodge touring car had no difficulty in catching him. One said, "I guess this has taught you a lesson." Cornell is reputed to have replied: "It sure has. Next time I'll use a faster car."

Bill Dangerfeld was that year's President of the Club, and also president of his influential family's mercantile business. He was seated next to the speaker's podium, looking as though he had just swallowed the worm in a bottle of mescal and wondered what would happen next.

Cornell was not known for tact and diplomacy, but for methods that got results. His talk was not long, but it was certainly instructive and informative. And impressive.

His beginning was low key: "Imagine a million square miles of lush tropical garden filled with lime, papaya, mango, coconut, avacado trees; bushes of bells, fresnos, anaheims, yellow hots and caribe peppers; pea vines and grapevines, cotton, opium poppies and marijuana.

"Picture this farmer's heaven, this elongated paradise lapped by the warm blue fish-filled waters of the Gulf of Lower California and the Pacific, and then visualize the United States as the great hungry market for all of that, with this Port the funnel through which it all flows.

"For shippers, brokers, importers, smugglers and tourists the day is 24 hours long and the load is getting heavier all the time. I think that some of you think that Customs Inspectors do nothing but sit on their duff and ask: '*Que trae?*' eight hours a day. But Inspectors not only have an increasing number of tourists and smugglers to contend with day and night, they have truckloads, trainloads, and

airplane loads of perishable merchandise that cannot be delayed.

"Besides all that, Customs Inspectors enforce the laws of 42 other departments, agencies, bureaus and divisions of the Federal government. Here at this Port we have a bare baker's dozen Inspectors to cope with all this business. They are worn out with overtime, so it is no wonder they get a little impatient with some of the folks who cross here. I freely admit some complaints are legitimate."

He paused. His face was getting red with some strong emotion. He drew a deep breath before going on.

"Take last night and a tired Inspector determined to protect the interest of the United States, as is his sworn duty and what he is paid to do, confronted by a smart aleck local man who should have known better who answered the Inspector's necessary questions with: 'I'm an American citizen but she is an unlawful Chinese and I'm bringing a load of contraband smoking opium in the trunk for her.' The woman, incidentally, was not his wife, who is out of town.

"The Inspector called in a female Customs employee to search the woman, who did have Oriental features, for identification, turned the car upside down and wrung it out. When he could find nothing to hold them on he let them go. Immediately the citizen hurried to the nearest telephone and complained angrily to his Senator of mistreatment at the border.

"The Senator got the Commissioner of Customs out of bed, he in turn called me and got me out of mine. He was irate and demanded that I transfer that Inspector where he wouldn't be exposing himself to the traveling public or better still, find a way to fire him for displaying such poor judgement.

"I was myself somewhat disturbed to be so rudely awakened and I called the Gate and questioned the Inspector's need to mistreat one of the border's most prominent people.

"He told me what had happened and asked me this: 'Suppose she really was an illegal alien and suppose there really was prohibited opium in the trunk? Collector, what would you have done?'

"He was exactly right. I called the Commissioner and told him so and if anyone was unhappy with my decision not to censure him in anyway, they should take it up with the man who appointed me — the President of the United States."

Collector Leap Cornell turned slowly and stared like an eagle about to swoop on his prey at Dangerfeld, whose fat face had gone pale, his eyes were bulging out of their sockets, and he looked like he was on the edge of a heart attack.

"It's not the judgement of the Inspector that is at issue here," Collector Cornell said. "Need I say more?"

Then he walked out.

Border Diplomacy

At one time each Customs Collection District was headed by a Collector, who usually lasted only as long as the existing administration if he didn't do anything criminal, such as one who burned down the Customhouse in an unsuccessful effort to conceal his removal of several pounds of gold bullion from Customs custody.

Most Collectors only showed up around headquarters to collect their pay and their principal duty, if there was one, seemed to be one of diplomacy, to smooth ruffled feathers of citizens who felt they had somehow been mistreated by Customs.

Each District was virtually autonomous, each Port in a District, led by a Deputy Collector, nearly so. The Ports in the Arizona District were—and are—from east to west: Douglas, Naco, Nogales, Sasabe, and Sonoyta—now Lukeville. Lochiel was a sub-port.

But each of the employees of each Port was a rugged individualist, and it took some kind of manager to run a District filled with characters. The boss of the Arizona District at the time involved here was Leap Cornell. He may have been the only Collector who actually knew anything about Customs, and nobody but he was going to be boss.

In order that he might be aware of what was going on at the various Ports in his District, Cornell made frequent visits to them, which was how he happened to be in Sasabe on a day there was a crossing of cattle on the hoof through the La Osa corrals and over the La Osa scales, which were right on the Line.

Cattle deals in Mexico can be complicated. An angry American buyer had just awakened to the fact that he had lost his shirt to a shrewd Mexican seller with no one to blame but himself and his thirst for tequila. In this particualr sale he found himself responsible for paying the per pound duty.

Because he wanted to pay as little as possible to offset the price he had finally agreed to pay for them, and to increase his ultimate profit after the steers were fattened and sold, he had starved and dehydrated them to reduce their weight before they reached the border. Some were so weak they had to be dragged onto the scale.

In order to save time it was customary for *vaqueros*, in this case paid for by the buyer, to cut the cattle into bunches of uniform size and rush them onto the scale. Duties were a cent and a half a pound for anything that weighed between 300 and 700 pounds, and outside those limits the duty was doubled. After the weight of a particular bunch was taken, they were counted off the scale and their number

CSP

divided into the scale weight to insure they were individually within the weight limits and entitled to the lower rate.

As this buyer kept trying to throw in one or two big or little ones in an effort to avoid paying the higher rate for them, Collector Cornell got tired of this and told the Deputy Collector to order *uno por uno*, a tactic which would cost the buyer more vaquero pay than he had anticipated, so this made him even more unhappy than he already was.

He was as obnoxious as nature, an overdose of tequila, and a hangover from the same could make such a man. He was loud and obscene in his criticism of Customs delay red tape, and insistently complained that the Deputy Collector was weighing heavy in favor of the Government. This was in the presence of customhouse brokers, veterinarians, honchos ram-rodding the crossing, and a few passersby who had nothing else to do but listen in.

Mister Leap Cornell waited for his Deputy to calm the man down or shoot him, and was ready to back him up in either case, but he ran out of patience and himself told the buyer in his own brand of diplomatic language to either shut his mouth and let the men get their paperwork done or get out.

The buyer mistook Cornell's mild manner for something else and said something to the effect that he should go off somewhere and practice an unnatural act upon himself.

"Up to now," said Mr. Cornell, "you were talking business. Now you just got personal." He took off his coat, laid his badge on the table, and jabbed a finger at the door. "Step out there in the road and I will show you the error of your ways."

They fought for awhile, sometimes on their feet, often on the ground, sometimes rolling into Mexico and back, and dust arose high above them. Finally, the buyer, curled around his sore crotch where a couple of Cornell's well-aimed kicks had connected, spilling blood and spitting teeth. After being revived by a bucket of water poured over him and half a bottle of tequila poured into him, with one ear hanging to his head by a thread of skin and one eye swelled shut, gazed up at Cornell respectfully through the other one and exclaimed: "Mithter Cornell, I never theen thuch fair Cuthtom weighth before."

The Confirmation of Ben Daniels

During his terms in office President Ronald Reagan had problems getting some of his appointees confirmed. This brings to mind another U.S. President who had similar difficulty: Teddy Roosevelt.

In 1884 Roosevelt went out to North Dakota to go into ranching. He became an admirer of a segment of frontier society, the rugged ranchers and cowboys who had adapted so well to an outdoor existence in fair weather or foul tending their land, cattle, and horses. He appreciated what he called "that delicious sense of equality" he found to be a characteristic of the old West.

Other characteristics of the American Westerners he met were their honesty, strength, and determination to win over adversity. So it followed that when the Spanish-American War came along he would want to recruit such men for service in the unit he formed.

His Rough Riders had to be tough. A Phoenix, Arizona newspaper in 1896 said, "Every member of the regiment must be able to ride the hardest bronc that ever bucked. He must furthermore be able to ride with the bridle reins in his teeth, with a revolver in each hand, and to drive nails in a board fence on each side of the road as his bronco flies along. That is all that will be required of him. He will be asked no embarrassing questions about his social standing, his politics, or his religion."

Ben Daniels was a member of the Rough Rider regiment. The tough, heroic man became well known to Roosevelt, and these two from totally different backgrounds formed a deep and lasting respect for each other.

When Roosevelt became President, Daniels was a deputy sheriff in recently-formed Santa Cruz County, working out of Nogales, Arizona, the county seat. He traveled to Washington to ask the President to make him Marshal of Arizona Territory.

Roosevelt looked with favor upon his request. He knew Ben Daniels was a good man and was determined that he should have the post in spite of expected opposition. Daniels was quite willing to have his background, character, and qualifications subjected to scrutiny in the investigative process. He had an impressive record in law enforcement. He had been Marshal of Dodge City during the turbulent days of that wild place. He was Night Marshal of Cripple Creek, Colorado, for two or three years, making a record as a peace officer not matched anywhere on the frontier, according to newspapers of the day. He kept the lawless element under tight rein in the rough Western towns where the atmosphere was nothing like

that in official Washington's social circles.

The opposition to his appointment as U.S. Marshal of Arizona focused on two issues. The first was a moral one.

The "careful" scrutiny of Daniels' past took a delaying period of five months. Evidence was turned up that indicated he might have been a gambler. This was offensive to some people. Others reminded them that Arizona Governor Nathan Oakes Murphy had been a faro dealer yet no one had objected to that appointment.

It was true that Daniels' life had not been spent in the quiet halls of academia, or in tranquil pursuit of a livelihood in merchandising or the ministry. He had earned high marks in the school of hard knocks and if examinations had been held in the art of gentility, Ben Daniels would not have received a very good grade.

His lack of experience in the fine art of social intercourse was not, however, the other issue. That reason for opposing his appointment was political: he was a Democrat. So when he was finally confirmed, it was a personal triumph for Roosevelt, who considered the Arizonan a diamond in the rough as he did so many of the friends he had made in the Dakotas.

About a year after his confirmation, Daniels was in Washington on businss. President Roosevelt invited him to lunch at the White House where he was also entertaining the British Ambassador.

The President was happy to be able to bring these two men together, for the Ambassador had expansive knowledge of the American West, which would give them all a common conversational ground.

By way of introduction Roosevelt said, "Mr. Ambassador, allow me to present my friend, Ben Daniels, Marshal of Arizona, of whom I am genuinely proud."

It is reported that Ben Daniels grasped the hand of King Edward's envoy to the United States of America with the firm grip of an ex-cowboy, lawman, miner and Rough Rider and while pumping it vigorously, said, "Ambassador, he ain't a damn bit prouder of me than I am of him."

M.A.D.D.

Everybody who crosses the border at Nogales is familiar with the Customs officer's refrain: "What are you bringing from Mexico?"

Dennis Ryan, the ex-bartender, approached the first car in the incoming lane at Grand Avenue Gate on his first day in his new job as a Customs Inspector, planted his well-kept hands on the sill of the driver's window, leaned forward, forgot everything he had been told to say and asked: "What'll it be, gents?"

Ryan was short on education but long on heart. He had not been the kind of bartender who would ply his customers with a drink if he knew they were going to drive, particulary if they were going to drive between Nogales and Tucson, through the Fifty-First State. He would more likely urge coffee on them and was a one-man originator of M.A.D.D., except that in his day the initials stood for Many Alcoholics Die Drunk.

It was Apaches who caused the road from the border to be known as El Camino del Diablo. After the advent of the automobile, after the twisting trace down the Santa Cruz River Valley was oiled, graveled and paved the name was changed to Camino de Muerte.

After a Nogales man was appointed to the Highway Commission and got some of the curves straightened out by bulldozers and dirt movers instead of drunk drivers the human carnage did not stop, but continued at a reduced rate considering increasingly greater numbers of border visitors.

In those times it was the generally accepted feeling in the Fifty-First that if a man or woman wanted to kill him or herself and sometimes his family through lethal ingestion of alcoholic beverages, it was their privilege. It was a free country.

So when a family of four with an inebriated member at the wheel drove off the road through the Patagonias between Nogales and Washington Camp and tumbled to a crunching halt 400 feet below, relatives and friends marched behind the four caskets to the cemetery on the hill weeping and wailing but saying, *"Asi es la vida."*

When a popular cowboy went over the edge in the Atascosas on the way to Ruby and didn't show up at home, searchers found him in a deep wash 12 hours later, lying in the battered remains of his ancient pickup with both legs and one arm broken, his pelvis out of position, and a terrible hangover.

It was a period during which if a man could walk from a bar stool to the seat of his car, even if he had to be helped behind the wheel, he was deemed capable of driving. An open bottle of tequila on the seat beside him was not cause for mandatory penalties and jail time.

CSP

Just such a driver steered his Nash sedan carefully into the incoming lane at Grand Avenue at three o'clock one morning with a 12-foot four by four protruding from the shattered windshield in front, extending through the car, and jutting out the smashed rear window.

"How in the world?" asked an amazed Inspector, "did you do that?"

"Do what?" the driver asked.

In the interest of preserving life and limb, U.S. border inspectors did what they could to stop the liquor-induced mayhem on the highways, but they had no clout outside the laws they were empowered to enforce.

A fresh, new, young Immigration Inspector pointed that out to Dennis Ryan one night as they were about to go off shift when Ryan delayed to sidetrack a drunken driver and take his key away.

"My dear sir," Ryan said politely, "I know that. I also know that you are a married man because I see your attractive wife coming to pick you up sometimes after work, with that pretty little girl of yours that is barely big enough to look over the dashboard with her eyes dancing when she sees her daddy."

"What has that got to do with what?" the new boy asked. "Here they come now."

"I know," Ryan said. "And suppose I had left that drunk driver go on through and he crashed head-on into your wife's car, sent the broken steering column slashing into her chest, and your little girl came smashing through the broken glass of the windshield face first—"

"Enough," the Immigration Inspector said. "You made your point."

The Executioners

In the early 1960's undeclared psittacine birds seized at the Port of Nogales were put to death because there were no facilities for quarantine to determine whether they had psittacosis, a parrot fever dangerous to man.

The Smiths from Phoenix were making their rum run—the monthly trip to Nogales for the then quota of a gallon of alcoholic beverages per person. They bought theirs at El Mickey Mouse and were returning to their car when they passed a sidewalk parrot vendor.

"Oh," said Mrs. Smith, "I want a parrot."

The peddler took a little one from its cage and transferred it from his finger to that of Mrs. Smith. The small bird allowed her to stroke its head and back, cooed at her charmingly, and she was immediately in love.

"Wait a minute," Mr. Smith said. "Isn't it illegal to cross these birds into the United States?"

"A technicality," said the salesman. "Don't tell the Inspector you have him."

"He would have to be blind not to see a bird as colorful as this."

"So hide him," the peddler said.

"What if he squawks?" Smith asked.

The peddler laid the bird in the crook of his arm, took a bottle from his pocket, dipped an eye dropper into it, extracted some clear fluid and put several drops into the bird's mouth. The bird began to snore gently.

"Amazing," Smith said. "What kind of tranquilizer is that?"

"No-see-em juice," said the vendor, and stuffed the bird into a brown sack. "The Inspector no see 'em if you tuck him under the front seat." He showed the label on the bottle to Smith, who read: "Tequila."

When the Smiths arrived at the Grand Avenue Gate, Customs Inspector Tony Russo was about to release them after their declaration when the bird woke up with an incredible hangover and let out a series of distressed squawks. Russo seized the bird because the Smiths had not included it in their declaration and because it was a restricted entry, and sent them on their way parrotless, out of pocket, and out of sorts.

He put the sacked bird on the cluttered top of a filing cabinet inside the garita and conveniently forgot it until after he was relieved by the earnest raw recruit, ex-bartender Dennis Ryan, and he was at home. Then he telephond the Shift Captain at the Grand Avenue

Gate and told him he had forgotten to terminate the bird.

"I'll bet," said the Shift Captain, well knowing the reluctance of Inspectors to be the agent of death for an unwitting accomplice to a violation of law. He put aside his newspaper and his mug of coffee and walked out to Dennis Ryan on the traffic lane.

"Look, Dennis," he said, "I am going to give you an opportunity to learn another important duty of Customs Inspectors."

"Thank you, Captain," said Ryan, "I appreciate that."

"There is a parrot in that brown paper sack on top of the filing cabinet. Take it out and kill it."

Ryan was aghast. "I can't do that to a helpless bird."

"Comes with the job," the Shift Captain said. "Nobody told you it would be easy."

He then explained to Dennis the reasons for destruction of the parrot. Ryan was not happy about the murderous assignment but was too good a soldier to disobey an order.

"How do I kill it?" he wanted to know.

"Painlessly and quickly. Start the engine of the government car parked behind the garita and pucker the mouth of the sack round the exhaust pipe."

Ryan walked inside, grabbed the sack, and slammed out. The Shift Captain went back to absorb his coffee and news until he was disturbed by the Immigration and Agriculture Inspectors complaining they had been doing Customs work for the last quarter of an hour.

He hurried behind the garita. Ryan was squatted on his heels at the rear of the car with the mouth of the paper sack tight around the exhaust pipe as instructed.

He said, "I'm burning my hands, Captain. When is this bird dead?"

"Conservatively," the Shift Captain said, "13 minutes ago."

Carefully Ryan took the sack away from the exhaust and peered inside. There was an indescribable look of disgust on his face when he tossed the sack to the Shift Captain and walked back to the traffic lane.

The Shift Captain looked into the sack. Nestled comfortably inside were an apple, a banana, and two sandwiches wrapped in wax paper.

To Dennis Ryan goes the credit for ending the practice of putting psittacine birds to death at Nogales, yet still preventing their entry. If a bird was declared, its owners were compelled to return it to Mexico. If it was undeclared, it was seized, the violators fined, and after they had left the Gate, the Inspector would carry it across the Line and give it to a Mexican celador or anyone else who would take it.

The Guajalote Ganga

In spite of the night time attractions across the Line in the Cavern, El Cid, the Concordia, Canal street, the town of Nogales, Arizona was like any small town anywhere. There was a tendency to fold up the sidewalks at ten and a 13-pound bowling ball could have rolled north from the border to the city limits without striking either a pedestrian or a vehicle.

This left a boring gap for Inspectors on the evening shift at the Gates from ten until midnight, which they tried to fill by telling lies to each other, crowding into the shelter booth between a couple of incoming lanes on Grand Avenue.

On a cold November evening Tony Russo took advantage of such an opportunity to start building his Thanksgiving laugh. The net he tossed caught Dennis Ryan, whom Russo had once successfully talking into investing in an acre of turkey tracks cheap with the assurance he would double his money in 30 days. He returned the money after it was learned that a flash flood had washed them out before they could be harvested.

The occasion was in a conversational lull between the Inspectors about the shortage of edible turkeys today and the high cost of those that were available. Dennis Ryan, who was to relieve Tony, came in just in time to hear Russo say: "I heard there is a carload of them in the railroad that will be sold tomorrow morning. Cheap."

All of those present had been worked over at least once by Tony Russo. They looked at each other knowingly and kept silent, but Dennis Ryan asked, "Why?"

"Something about demurrage," Russo said. "And a law that perishables have to be delivered or sold within a certain period of time. They ought to go pretty cheap, and fast. A real *ganga.*"

When Russo went out to get into his car and go home he remembered a big cardboard carton in the trunk. He had picked it up at Puchi's Progressive because his wife, Fina, had asked him to bring it home to pack some stuff in. He took it back to Dennis and said, "There is a limit of three turkeys to a customer so you better take this with you to carry them in."

In the morning as soon as Dennis was relieved he hurried with the box to the railroad yard. The car was right where Russo had said it would be, parked alongside the switch shanty in front of the Courthouse at the Court Street crossing. He took up a positon right under the door, and was standing there when Leap Cornell, on his way to his office in the Customs District headquarters which was then in the Post Office, paused in his long black seized Buick and yelled, "Hey, Dennis, watcha doin'?"

"Big turkey ganga soon as they open up, Collector," Dennis said. "Want I should get one for you?"

Leap Cornell left his Buick purring on the crossing and walked over. "Where'd you hear about them?"

"Tony Russo."

Cornell hadn't a gullible bone in his body and he knew Russo well. He reached up and swung the car door open. It was empty.

Ryan said, "Damn, they musta opened early and sold 'em already."

Cornell walked back to his car, shaking his head, wondering if he could have made a mistake in bringing Dennis out from behind the bars and giving him a job in Customs.

Ryan finally got the feeling that maybe he had been had, but said nothing to anybody. A few days later it was he who had the four-to-midnight shift and Tony Russo who relieved him, which he did just as a battered pickup pulling an equally beatup travel trailer drew into the incoming lane.

Maybe Russo was feeling contrite, more likely it was just his way, at any rate he said to Ryan, "Go on home, Dennis, I'll handle this one."

The driver of the pickup proved to be a garrulous old gentleman who was aching to tell somebody who could understand him about the finest fishing trip he had ever had in his life. He had been on the waters of the Sea of Cortez for several days, but never in them. He smelled like dried codfish.

Russo went about his work, looking first in the camper on the back of the pickup while the old man talked with Ryan, who was too polite to walk off. When Russo came out of the camper he told the old man to open the trailer which he did without even looking at Russo or stopping talking while he unlocked a padlock and stood aside to let Russo step inside. He was so absorbed in his story he wasn't even aware of what he was doing.

Ryan interrupted him gently to ask if he intended to drive all the way home tonight.

"Yep." the old man said. "I got double tanks and I filled them with that cheap Mexican gasoline. I'm driving straight on, no reason to stop anywhere."

Quietly, Ryan closed the trailer door and snapped the lock. He said, "Well, sir, have a good trip."

The old man said, "Thanks a lot," got into the pickup and drove off, leaving only the smell of burned Mexican gasoline and an odor of salt-cured fish.

Dennis Ryan walked into the garita and picked up the phone.

"Rosita," he said, "could you bring me a sandwich? I'll be working Tony's shift. He's on his way to Colorado."

The Jack of Clubs

He was a Mexican *Celador* and the American Customs people at Nogales called him Californio because he had come from Tijuana. He was not a very nice man and looked the part, being non-smiling, mean, and ornery. He was in the habit of getting drunk and then defying anybody to take his gun away.

He was known to be a smuggler of goods both ways, and when he approached the border in the export lane where Dennis Ryan was on duty, Dennis stopped him on general principles and asked what he was taking to Mexico.

"*Nada, por supuesto, cantinero,*" said Californio, referring to Ryan's former occupation as bartender in his salutation.

"*Sin embargo,*" Ryan said, "*tengo que ver lo que trae en la petaca.*"

Complaining all the way, Californio got out and opened the trunk. In it were two bale-pressed cartons of dry goods valued at $700. Ryan promptly seized car and goods from the expostulating, surly Californio, who was deeply resentful.

The strange thing about this seizure was that the goods could be legally exported by the simple presentation of an export declaration. But because Customs officers of both countries generally give each other "freedom of the port", Californio thought he wouldn't bother. His primary consideration, though, was to avoid paying his fellow officers *mordida* or customs duty.

Ryan wasn't sure the Collector would back him, but should have known better: Leap Cornell backed his men, right or wrong, and he backed this one as a violation of the Export Control Act and ordered forfeiture of the goods. Ryan didn't expect to hear any more about it, but did. Owners of the car and merchandise sued for their release. The store on Morley Avenue where the goods had been bought were equally interested in recovering the goods, and they furnished counsel, a noted lawyer specializing in Customs and International law.

So the Customs Agency Service prepared the case for prosecution. And a couple months later, Ryan was subpoenaed to appear in Federal Court in Tucson.

As seizing officer he would testify about the seizure, and the Custodian of Seized Merchandise would testify that the goods had been turned over to him by Ryan and were in his custody. They rode to Tucson with Ted Street, the Customs Agent who had prepared the case.

They had a pre-trial appointment in the office of the Assistant

U.S. Attorney with George O'Hara, an assistant U.S. Attorney. O'Hara assured them they could rely on being held over for another day. So they got rooms at the Roskruge Hotel.

Then O'Hara dropped a bombshell on them when the case was called. He stood up and said, "Your Honor, in this case I have been advised by the client's attorney that he has not had an opportunity to apprise his clients of the date of this trial because they are in Mexico. He asks for a continuance."

The judge said, "Four months hence. Witnesses are free to go."

As they left the courtroom Street said, "Now you tell us. Well, we've got rooms, we might as well stay even though we'll have to pay for them out of our own pockets. O'Hara, come on up this evening. We'll have a game."

O'Hara declined, so did the siezure clerk, so Street and Ryan wound up in a game with a Swedish masseuse and a bellman in the Swede's room.

Things weren't going at all well except with the Swede, who had almost all their money, when Street got up and went to the water-cooler and drew a drink. When he sat down again the Swede drew a nickel out of the pot.

Street said, "What's that for?"

Swede said, "I don't get that water for nothing."

Street's face got red. "Why you cheap so and so," he said, "you already have all our money."

After he calmed down they continued playing, he and Ryan winning just often enough to stay in the game.

Later, they were playing "paco", a game similar to stud, but with every other card down. Ryan had four clubs in sight, the Swede had a couple of possibilities and he kept bumping Ryan up. Ryan was just stubborn enough to chance being wiped out in favor of winning a huge pot.

Street was dealing and it was down to Ryan and the Swede when Ryan happened to see the card on the bottom of the deck that Street was dealing from. It was the Jack of Clubs. Ryan didn't think anything more about it until it turned up in his hand.

The Swede was lucky he had pulled out the nickel earlier, that was about all he wound up with.

On the way back to Nogales the next day, Street said comfortably, "If we could have gotten O'Hara in a game, he would have paid for our rooms, but the Swede's money is as good as his. Besides, he made me mad."

An International Incident

His face was grooved with crevices and his friends called him *Cara de Mapa.* He was not the best-dressed Immigration Inspector on the Line, but he was a fine human being with a good sense of humor who could defuse the most serious situation and turn it into comedy, and his fellow Inspectors enjoyed working with him.

His boss, Elmo Dahl, Immigration Officer in Charge, thought that if there was any place that dignity should be preserved it was at the border. He had been a military man and distanced himself from the help as far as he could. He thought people like Mapa belonged anywhere but in a service where he was the first American that visitors to our country saw.

The United States was helping put Japan back on its feet after WW II when three Japanese Immigration officials traveling with a State Department escort arrived at Nogales. Dahl didn't question why that island empire needed to look at a border operation, so with his help they were permitted to enter Mexico even though they had neither visas for that country nor re-entry permits for the United States.

They were still across the Line when Mapa came on shift, a little late because his depth of vision having outreached the length of his arms, he had just been fitted with a pair of glasses that vanity dictated he keep concealed as long as possible. Today he wore a brand new uniform, he had donated the threadbare and patched old one to Bulla, the disadvantaged Mexican who had no source of income except solicitation of subsistence funds from sympathetic people such as the border inspectors.

At 5:00 p.m. Dahl came to the Gate, straight-backed, brush cut, and expressed surprise and displayed pleasure when he saw Mapa in his new garb.

"Tonight of all night," he said, "you must make a fine impression." He told him about the Japanese. "They have a letter of permission from me to re-enter. When they come, pick it up from the State Department's man. And for goodness sake, observe proper decorum. We want to give a good impression of the United States Immigration Service as we represent it here on the Mexican border."

Cara de Mapa said, 'I will treat them like visiting royalty. I will take off my cap, bow until my forehead touches the ground, and graciously wave them on their way."

"Exactly what I don't want you to do," Dahl said as he walked away shaking his blonde crew cut.

Cara de Mapa took a seat on a stool where he could work

vehicular traffic and foot travelers at the same time. No sooner was he comfortable than the car containing the Japanese arrived. The State Department man handed Mapa Dahl's letter.

Cara de Mapa looked at the car's occupants. They were all staring up at him through black-rimmed glasses, which reminded him of those he had just picked up that day, and he took them from his pocket. The case the optometrist had put them in was the soft kind that the lenses slip into, then a flap is pulled down and snapped to hold them securely. The temples folded over the flap to make a compact package for easy pocket storage.

Cara de Mapa fumbled the temples of the new glasses open and fitted them over his ears, neglecting to remove the case.

"My God!" he shouted, staggering to his feet, "I've gone blind."

The Customs Shift Captain and the Customs Inspector exploded with spontaneous laughter, which tended to calm Mapa down and with dignity, he removed the glasses from their case, put them on, and perused the letter.

A hungry Bulla chose that moment to arrive on the scene, coming across the Line to stand at attention beside Cara de Mapa, proudly wearing the discarded old uniform complete with cap so big for him it hid his ears and his eyes.

The Japanese stared solemnly at this new Inspector, a toothless dirty-faced man wearing no shirt under a uniform jacket that hung to his knees, with the sleeves turned back to the elbow so his hands could be free, and with the pants rolled up to expose blackened bare feet to the ankle.

He extended a grimy hand and began an unmelodious song for his dinner. Frantically, Cara de Mapa searched the pockets of his new uniform for money. Finding none, he appealed to his co-workers: "Give him something and get him out of here."

The kind-hearted Customs Inspector, Dennis Ryan, dropped a couple of coins in Bulla's hand and he scampered away. And in order to save what remnant of decorum remined, Cara de Mapa doffed his cap, bowed deeply, and waved the visitors on.

By the time the story got back to Dahl it had been so deformed it wore little relation to what had actually happened, which was already funny enough. Dahl went around so angry that his face was red for a week, trying to think up ways to get Cara de Mapa legally dismissed from the Service. But by that time Washington had learned of their mistakes in puttting a man like Dahl in charge of such a group as the independent border inspectors, and transferred him to headquarters where they could bury him in the bureaucracy.

Love on the Babocomari

Cara Mapa and Will Benson, the white-headed Sheriff of Santa Cruz wearing the holster full of pipes instead of the Smith and Wesson 44-40 he had carried to tame the county with, were kids over on the Babocomari River where their respective sires owned adjoining ranches.

Sometimes the Sheriff would drop in on the boys at the Line for a cup of coffee and conversation. If Cara de Mapa happened to be on duty the conversaion was a whole lot more entertaining than whatever was happening in the traffic lanes.

Sheriff would come in the door of the garita and yell something like: "Mapa, you ever sleep with a redhead?" and Mapa would holler back, "Not a goddam wink."

Then Mapa might say, "What he's aching to tell you is—"

We had this Morgan stallion known all around Cochise County for never missing the target. Name was Wichita. So here comes Sheriff's daddy, ole man Benson, with this dainty pinto mare he wants bred to our Wichita. Me and Will here want to go fishin down on the River and my Ole Man says we can after we take Daisy down to the corrals and turn her in with Wichita.

He takes the Sheriff's Ole Man into the house to polish off a bottle of *bacanora* and we lead dainty Daisy down to the corrals where Wichita stops chompin hay to paw the earth and snort at Daisy, only Daisy seems more interested in the proud-cut stud next door.

Wichita suddenly runs a kickin and a jumpin around his corral and we're watching him and payin no attention to ole Jack, our Missouri donkey pawin manure in his own corral when we lead Daisy to the gate into Wichita's.

Sheriff here skins out in front of Daisy to open it, then yells: "LOOK OUT!" and scampers up the fence like a chased squirrel up a saguaro tree. I look around just as that old Jack busts out of his corral in a shower of wood splinters with all his teeth showin and his jock hangin an plowin up the ground and I know if anything gets in his way it's going to get tromped on so I hang onto Daisy's rope and climb up beside Will just as ole Jack lands on top of her.

When ole Jack is done he drops out of her and no more interested in her goes back to his own corral and takes to chompin hay while Daisy just stands there lookin dreamy into space, ever once in awhile a-sighin and a-shiverin. I lead her into Wichita's corral where she kicks his face when he tries to nuzzle her, an me an Sheriff here race out fishing, leaving 'em together an hopin for the best.

After awhile we hear my Ole Man callin an we hurry back, get Daisy and tie her to the back of Ole Man Benson's pickup. They go

rattlin down our lane, Daisy trotting behind with that far-away expression still on her face.

A few months later, here comes Sheriff's daddy racin up our country lane a hunnert miles an hour with the yellow dust pluming out behind. I get a feeling all is not too well and slide off to the barn's hayloft where I can peek out and listen.

Ole Man Benson brings the pickup to a sliding halt in front of the house. My Ole Man comes to the porch.

"Well," he calls out, "that Daisy mare musta foaled by now. Come on in and we'll knock back another bottle of bacanora to celebrate."

"You and your goddam bacanora," Ole Man Benson yells, shaking his fist up at my Ole Man. "Foal she did and she dropped the ugliest goddam pinto mule in 17 counties and I want my money back."

After he calms down and goes home I hear my Ole Man calling. I go down with my tail between my legs expecting the worse. When I get to him he unbuckles his belt and starts to pull it through the loops and I know I'm in for a real good one.

Then he starts to laughing and falls down and rolls around the ground, laughing so hard he can't get his belt off and gives up on that idea.

When he stops laughing he says, "I knowed what happened minute I seen them bits of broken wood off ole Jack's corral, but I figure I'd keep quiet an hope for the best."

Then he puts his arm around my shoulders and we go inside where he gave me my first belter of bacanora.

"An you ain't stopped beltin it down since, either," Sheriff said, "an that's the God's truth."

Then he says, "But what I was about to tell you is this one—"

Too Big To Miss

They started calling him Long John when he reached six-feet-six, where he stopped growing up and started to grow sideways. When he was 22 years old he rode up San Juan Hill with the 1st U.S. Volunteer Cavalry, an awesome giant on a horse as large as an elephant.

He was too big a target to miss, so he was carrying an extra pound of lead when they carried him down. A little later he gained more weight when they pinned a Congressional Medal of Honor to his chest.

He did some cowboying on a big ranch between the Santa Rita Mountains in Pima County and the Whetstones in Cochise in Arizona but saw no future in it. In early 1905 he rode to Tucson and applied for a job as a Line Rider for the United States Customs Service.

A couple days later he wrote a laborious note that read: "Dear Teddy I want to work for the government but the Collector at Tucson says I can't pass the test, yours truly, Long John Silber."

A few days after that the Collector at El Paso, who was in charge

of Tucson, got a letter on White House stationery that read: "I would rather have for a Customs Mounted Patrolman a fellow who can read a smuggler's trail, follow it to the end and bring him in than a fellow who reads good but doesn't know which end of the gun a bullet comes out of. Put Long John Silber to work."

Long John Silber was still stationed at Montana Camp down on the border when Leap Cornell began his first term as Collector of Customs for the District of Arizona. Long John was 68 years old, still riding a regular patrol on a white mare, the only animal in the county large enough to carry him.

Leap Cornell worried that John was getting too old, might fall off his horse out in the hills and not be able to make it in. He suggested to John that he was entitled to hang up his spurs.

"Mr. Cornell," Long John said in his slow way of talking, "the guvnment's been good to me an' I'm goin' to give it all I got."

A few days before his 70th birthday, the mandatory retirement age, he rolled his heavy body out of his sagging side of the bed. Alice breathed softly on the high side, not stirring. He shuffled stiffly and barefoot to the kitchen and started a fire in the cook stove.

The scent of coffee boiling was in the air before he finished shaving and went out to the kitchen again. He filled a blue pottery mug and

clumped quietly to the front porch, picking his old brass telescope from a shelf on the way.

Dawn was graying the sky above Mule Ridge Mountain as he eased his bulk into a complaining old chair and waited for the day to become light enough to use the glass.

Sunshine creeping into dark canyons began to disperse night's shadows as he finished his coffee. His big fists held the spyglass steady as he moved it in easy motion, doing what he did every morning, sweeping the peaks and valleys as familiar to him as the back of his hand, looking for anything out-of-the-ordinary.

This morning he found it in a sad-faced rat-colored burro standing dejectedly in a clearing on top of a little knoll a mile off, less than a mile from the border. Two bright new five-gallon cans were lashed to its packsaddle.

He knew that animal belonged to a no-good woodcutter he had arrested several times with smuggled mescal, a mean-eyed man it wouldn't do to turn your back on. Each of those times he had taken him to headquarters in the machine where Chief Inspector Adams fined him and turned him over to Immigration because he was an *alambrista.* Once, they put him in jail for a year and a day, he would be just through with his sentence, Long John figured.

Long John figured him to be sleeping rolled up in a blanket under a nearby tree. In the front room he lifted his gunbelt off a peg in the wall by the door, slapped his old gray hat on his head, tugged on boots and walked out quietly, so as not to waken Alice.

The husky white mare stood hipshot, dozing with her velvet nose barely against a rail of the corral fence. He warmed the bit in his hands before he slipped it into her mouth gently, placed a thick blanket on her back carefully, swung the saddle high enough that the stirrup cleared the sleepy animal, cinched it with a powerful tug, opened the gate and led her out.

He knew exactly where to turn off the road down California Gulch to guide the mare into a little meadow at the base of the knoll. He dismounted, stifling the grunts of pain of arthritic joints, and started up the hill, walking quietly, using oak, juniper, manzanita, and rock outcrops as cover to keep between him and the top of the hill.

He was crawling softly on centuries-old leaf mold under the trees when he reached the top of the bald knoll across from where he had seen the burro. It was gone.

Like a great, curious grizzly he stood up slowly. The bullet whistled across the knoll and hit him in the chest.

Long John Silber gave all he was able to the "guvnment" that had been so good to him.

Undeclared, Restricted, or Prohibited

It was frequently two days late in arriving from Mexico City but they called it the *rapido* anyway. Its powerful steam locomotives dragged a dozen coaches and two Pullman cars right up to the border fence separating Mexico from the United States, where the depot most conveniently used to be. Coach passengers disembarked and followed *cargadores* pushing baggage-laden hand trucks through an Immigration check at Grand Avenue in Nogales, then up to the Customs Inspection Room at the rear of the Federal building on International Avenue. Here, Inspectors dozing in the sun in chairs tilted back against the wall moaned awake at this interruption of their siesta, got up groaning and perfunctorily performed the Customs examination.

The only training the first new Inspectors to be hired in a decade got was a couple of weeks in the Inspection Room followed by two more on the graveyard shift on Grand Avenue. It was generally conceded that it took five years of on-the-job training to make a good Inspector. Les Wisdom, who held a temporary indefinite appointment, felt the war would not last long enough for him to make himself the indispensable man at that rate, and was determined to cram all the Customs lore in that he could as fast as possible in the hope of getting a permanent assignment just in case somebody did not come back from WW II. He watched other Inspectors so intently as they performed their duties that they thought he was a spy out of the Bureau of Customs, but even that fear didn't influence their efficiency any.

What he learned in the two weeks he was at the Inspection Room before they put him out on the Line could be summed up in the three words he spoke when pawing his way through the baggage of an irritated coach passenger who asked, "What are you looking for, anyway?" In general, Wisdom knew he was looking for undeclared, restricted, and prohibited items but there were so many of them he could not be specific, so replied honestly, "I don't know."

Chief Randolph Adams had presented Wisdom with a gun and a holster and a mandate not to fire it unless he was being shot at, but nobody had shown him how to use it. He could not even practice with it because they gave him only five loads and his $1860 per annum salary would not permit frivolous expenditures like even the cost of a box of home made wadcutters.

So when they teamed him with the white-headed tobacco-chewing

Immigration Inspector Bob Boomer, who operated a chicken farm in the daytime and caught up on his sleep on permanent graveyard at night, he was as poorly prepared as if they had just recruited him off the street.

They were sitting on a bench on the concrete platform that supported the blocky Grand Avenue garita when Boomer stood up, stretched, said, "Think you can handle it now?"

Confident, Wisdom said, "Sure. Where are you going?"

"Inside to catch some sleep if you'll get off my bed."

Wisdom stood, Boomer lifted the bench, shoved it under the counter in the garita. Wisdom was then treated to the unique spectacle of a six-foot, 180 pound Immigration Inspector with chicken feathers clinging to the seat of his green 12-ounce worsted pants curled up on his side on a four-foot bench, face to the wall, invisible to the casual passersby.

Boomer's snores quicky settled into a steady rhythm that was about to put Wisdom to sleep himself when an Essex sedan drew into the traffic lane from Mexico and a man darted past it into the United States on winged feet.

Wisdom reacted quickly. Recalling something he had read in the laws or regulations governing the authorities of a Customs Inspector about calling on any person within a radius of two miles for help if needed, he jumped on the running board of the Essex, yelled at the driver, "Catch that man," grabbed his cap and hung on.

The illegal entrant was running full out when Wisdom dropped on him, tore a hole in the knee of his own uniform pants, lost his cap in the darkness and knocked as much wind out of himself as out of his target. His commandeered car vanished north into the night.

The *alambrista* offered no resistance as Wisdom, rather pleased with the way he had handled the situation, led him back to the garita. Boomer woke up smacking his lips as though he had the taste of chicken manure in his mouth, voluntarily deported the illegal alien back to Mexico without bothering with documentation, took some of the cockiness out of Wisdom when he said, "You should'n'a'lef' your post of duty," stuffed a fresh wad of snuff in his lip, curled up on the bench again and went back to sleep.

More of Wisdom's cockiness disappeared when, a half-hour later, the phone rang: the Immigration Border Patrol back-up station at Amado, 30 miles down the road to Tucson.

"Just pulled two aliens out of an Essex sedan. They say you passed them through the Gate."

Wisdom might not have been well-informed yet about Customs and Immigration procedures, but he was St. Louis street-smart. "No

Essex passed through on my shift," he lied, and hung up quickly.

He wasn't just covering for Boomer either, for it had suddenly occurred to him that if there were illegal aliens there might also have been a load of undeclared, restricted, or prohibited goods in the car as well.

Snake in the Grass

Les Wisdom, the temporary-indefinite war-time Inspector of Customs, was not a veteran of any wars. His 4-F classification kept him out of WW II which was something Chief Inspector Randolph Adams could not forgive him for, particularly after that other war-time recruit, Billy Cardwell, was drafted.

Nor could he get used to Wisdom's flippancy. Adams had been in the Navy even before World War I and sometimes mentioned those days when "We were iron men in wooden ships." Innocently, Wisdom would say, "Isn't that the other way around, Randy?"

Then the Chief would get red all over his thin grey face and trot off muttering, mostly because none of his subordinates had ever called him "Randy" before. Only the fact that Wisdom made more seizures than all the other Inspectors combined kept the Chief from taking some kind of drastic action.

Wisdom was sensitive about his defect and that accounted for an exaggerated machismo. An early life on a Kansas harvester crew had layered a strong, though small, frame with powerful muscle, but dust and chaff had weakened his lungs. The mail-order uniform he wore hid his strength so adequately that some unwary newcomers to the Border force, challenging him during dull moments in the traffic flow just for the hell of it, were surprised to find themselves quickly out-wrestled.

So he was a kind of cocky little King of the Mountain around the Gates when a stocky ex-Customs Patrolman named Andrew Lee transferred from the northern border to Gate duty at Nogales.

Chief Adams thought it was time Wisdom was being taken down a peg or two. He knew something of the ex-patrolman's background that others didn't, and to the discomfiture of his Inspectors he took to hanging around the Gate trying to nudge Wisdom into a confrontation with Andrew Lee.

It finally happened. Wisdom should earlier have recognized the signs but didn't until one day he was lying on his back in the traffic lane staring up at Andy Lee and wondering what horse had just kicked him. Then he noticed that Andy's ears resembled cauliflower balls and his nose was flat and broad across the bridge.

Chief Adams laughed harder than the rest, which was a momentous event, for he had never been known to laugh out loud before. He said, "Montana Lee was a professional wrestler before he got some sense squeezed into his head and joined the Patrol."

Wisdom's philosophy was, "Don't get mad, get even." It took a little time.

He was working in the secondary inspection area, inside its garita, morosely watching through one-way glass as some Customs Agents shook down some clean-cut college kids when he saw one student edge over to a GI garbage can and drop something under its not-wholly closed lid. Only a few minutes before, Wisdom had seen the janitor empty the *basura* from that same can.

He sauntered outside and stood by until the Agents conceded their information must have been poor and were about to release the students, then lifted the garbage can lid to expose the only thing in its 33-gallon emptiness: a box that had once contained kitchen matches but now held a full load of manicured marijuana and some seeds.

Wisdom secretly transferred a few seeds to his own pocket before the agents took the evidence, arrested the students, and seized their car.

If the Customs Inspectors, relaxed in their chairs on the loading dock propped against the wall of the Inspection Room, had been observant or even curious, they would have noticed that for the next couple of months Les Wisdom was around the Inspection Room a lot, whether he was assigned there or not. They would have noticed that he would often stand on the dock sipping water from a tall glass and just sort of gazing into space like a ruminating cow. Then he would toss whatever remained of water in his glass onto a patch of bermuda growing in front of the dock, and return the glass to his locker.

Collector Leap Cornell only came that way twice a year, walking up the ramp to the dock Chief Adams and the others traveled several times daily. His semi-annual visit came two months after Wisdom's embarrassment at the hands of Andy Lee. He paused on his way up the ramp, looking down, then nodded to the Inspectors who had jumped to their feet when he drove into the compound and walked into the Chief's office.

Moments later the Chief charged out with his narrow face scarlet to stand where Les Wisdom usually stood when sipping his tall glassful of water. He bent over and tugged at the top of a weed that had grown almost to the level of the dock, pulled it out of the ground, hurled it to the concrete under his feet and stomped the life out of it like it was a dangerous snake while glaring bug-eyed at his unobservant—or collusive—Inspectors.

The Inspectors, expecting Cornell to come apart in some similarly spectacular manner, searched desperately for a place to hide.

The Collector merely walked past and got into his car. But as he drove away, Inspectors saw him suddenly bend over and pound the steering wheel, and his gust of roaring laughter drifted back as he drove out of sight.

Pancho Cupid

No tale of the Mexican border would be complete without some reference to the prominent revolutionary, Doroteo Arango aka Pancho Villa, an occasional visitor to Nogales, sometimes welcomed, sometimes not, and his unintentional contribution to the happiness of one Customs officer.

It happened in a roundabout way:

In 1913, Francisco Madero, President of Mexico, was assassinated and Victoriano Huerta took his place as Chief of State. The murder put Villa on the move. Again.

On the 13th of March, Nogales residents on International Avenue, Crawford Street Hill, and Nelson Avenue awoke to the sound of rifle fire as Villistas attacked the Federal garrison in Nogales, Sonora. By nightfall the garrison had fallen, but during that period from dawn to dusk, Americans in Arizona suffered a number of casualties from stray bullets.

And all that day, Customs Inspectors carried on "business as usual" right in the middle of the action.

A year later, Villa showed up again at Nogales. He, accompanied by 50 personal guards, his *estado mayor* and their mounts, crossed the border and were entertained by the officers of the 12th United States Infantry stationed at Camp Stephen D. Little (named, ironically enough) for a private who had been killed by a strayed bullet during Villa's former visit. Their host was General Black Jack Pershing, and among his officers was then 1st Lt. George S. Patton, Jr.

Not long after that, Villa and his troops became *persona non grata* in the U.S. Ammunition, which until then had been shipped to both Villistas and Federalistas to shoot at each other, was abruptly cut off for Villa, which put him in a bind.

Not in a conciliatory mood, he began to harass Americans in Mexico. Tension mounted along the border, so the American military moved in to help U.S. Customs keep the peace.

In November, 1915, a Villa supporter fired a shot across the Line and pulled the plug on the First Battle of Nogales. Customs officers, conducting business as usual again, spent much of their time ducking in and out of the garita, dodging screaming ricochets. Fifty Villistas were killed and two Americans died. Many were wounded in the shower of bullets that fell on both sides of the border.

So Villa was retaliating when on March 9 of 1916, he swooped in on border Columbus, New Mexico, 200 miles east of Nogales. He was looking to collect some munitions due him or extract their value from the hide of the gun merchant, Samuel Ravel, who had

GOD
HAPP

mishandled the deal.

The attack took place on the blackest of nights, which was fitting, because it was one of the blackest moments in U.S. history since the Civil War: 500 armed men from a foreign country attacked 300 Americans on American soil as they slept.

American intelligence was not very good even then. Although the garrison at Columbus was aware that Villa was on the move, and even that he intended to attack the town, they had no idea where he was or when he intended to attack. So the commanding officer stretched most of the soldiers under him out at strategic crossings along the boundary as a thin first line of defense, keeping only a skeleton force to protect the town.

He went to sleep secure in the belief that nothing could pass his perimeter troops, so it was a bit of a surprise and a rude awakening when Villa's 500 men drifted across the border and ghosted between detachments to hit Columbus like a two-tined pitchfork at three o'clock in the morning. One of the tines aimed at the depleted Fort Furlong on the edge of town, the other speared into the central section and put the torch to a city block of highly flammable buildings.

Among these was the two-story Commercial Hotel. Villistas raced through the halls, in and out of flames, killing four of the nine guests and the proprietor, Bill Ritchie. They stripped rings from the fingers of his sudden widow and bereaved daughters where they huddled in a room on the second floor and then departed before they got their serapes singed, leaving the ladies to roast in the flames.

Now up the blazing staircase bounded rescue in the form of a Unted States Customs officer. He led the frightened ladies through the leaping tongues of searing fire, from the hot crushng danger of falling roofs and collapsed walls into the dubious safety of the darkness outside where singing, smashing bullets criss-crossed streets and open spaces between buildings as the Villistas and Americans exchanged live deadly ammunition.

In that early morning action, 17 Americans were killed. Many were injured. Villa got neither arms, ammunition, nor the hide of the gun dealer, but fled southward back to Mexico.

In dawn's light, pursuing Americans found 167 Mexicans dead and ten wounded.

The happy spin-off from the night's tragedy was that Myrtle, Bill Ritchie's daughter, and the intrepid U.S. Customs officer were married. She became Mrs. Jolly Garner, sister-in-law of the man who 17 years later became the 32nd Vice President of the United States, John Nance Garner.

An Unexpected Climax (Rated R)

Graciela Garcia, aka Sugarfoot, was a wrinkle-faced dark-complected old lady with black hair streaked with grey. There were only a couple of teeth left in her flexible mouth, but she showed them often in a wide and knowing grin at the Customs Inspectors when she crossed the Line, which she did a dozen times a day.

Her uniform was a long grey dress that hung down to her ankles, many sizes too big for her. Her feet, clothed in worn, torn, and dusty tennis shoes with strings unlaced, protruded at right angles from under the hem of her dress. Her odd way of walking caused Inspectors to name her Sugarfoot, and if there was ever a witch contest in Nogales she would have won it going away.

She would approach the border from Mexico with that long dress hanging like a tent on her skinny body, but when she crossed back she looked like a candidate for a fat farm, for under the shift a dozen brand new dresses would be layered on her thin body, and on her head might be a half-dozen men's hats, because Mexican customs laws provided that anything a person wore was free of duty. She was doing the only work available to her at this sad time in her life. She was a merchandise mule.

Customs Inspector Bob Underhill and she went far back together. In fact, Underhill could claim he had turned her life around dramatically.

She was once one of the most beautiful women on the border, each part of her voluptuous figure fitted to its neighbor with such exact nicety that the effect was as stimulating as the most powerful aphrodisiac. When she walked across the Line on her way to work at the Paris Villa department store, every Inspector stopped whatever he was doing (if anything), to undress her with his eyes, tongue hanging out and saliva dripping from it like a sweating dog. She would flop her smile saucily around, bounce her twin beauties a little, grind her hips and could have been pulling a red ricksha with two undocumented Chinese and a load of smoking opium and nobody would have noticed.

One time the first of the three wives Underhill eventually had was in Texas visiting relatives. He had made some new friends over on the Canal during her absence and as she would be returning in a day or two he crossed the Line after work to bid them goodbye.

He was caught by the stop signal in front of the under-construction Fray Marcos de Niza Hotel, forced to halt halfway into the crosswalk, happening to be right in front of Graciela. He opened

the passenger side door of his VW Bug to apologize and she stepped right in, managing to draw one of her magnificent globes along his arm as he was closing the door.

So he gallantly suggested a relaxing ride into the country south of Nogales and she heartily endorsed the idea. They wended their way through traffic on Avenida Obregon and out of town on the highway to Hermosillo.

He knew of an isolated place, reached by a rutted road that wound eastward through an oak grove, a road that led to a hidden spot sometimes used by local sportsmen to sight in their deer rifles because its seclusion was ideal for that purpose.

The limbs of the trees they passed attested to another use to which the area had been put, being festooned with used condoms and bits of torn rayon undergarments, and before he had steered the VW down into an arroyo and stopped on a carpet of deteriorating *condones*, Graciela had the Underhill family jewels in her soft hands.

There followed a period of steady manipulation toward the ultimate objective, which was achieved in an unbelievable togetherness that rocked the car, tore holes in the roof, threw dust, dirt and gravel around them in a concerted explosion that climaxed in a shriek like that of tearing metal, of bits and pieces whining off into space with fading shrieks.

Graciela's head was back, eyes closed and lips parted, but Underhill, recovering quickly, backed the VW roaring up out of the arroyo with its wheels churning, shouting at the top of his lungs and honking his horn.

As they went speeding and bouncing back to the highway Graciela said, "I feel like that, too. Nobody, but nobody, has ever done me so good before, Roberto."

He thought it unnecessary to tell her that an unexpected rifleman must have considered the visible white top of his car that of an abandoned vehicle in the arroyo and warmed his gun barrel on it before getting down to serious shooting.

He concluded that it was a search for a repeat of such a perfect union that led Graciela Garcia to find work on Canal Street where her proficiency became legend, until age forced her to change positions.

Viva el Presidente!

Will Snyder Garcia had only worked for the Southern Pacific for a short time but had already been a gandy dancer, a baggage handler, baggage master, and freight agent. When he became a traveling auditor he was convinced he had a beautiful future.

Conviction became certainty with an invitation to join the Vice-President and General Manager of the Southern Pacific of Mexico, Leap Cornell, the Collector of Customs, and the Chief Customs Inspector in a game in the VP's private business car parked behind the City Hall in Nogales, Arizona. It had red carpets and drapes, overhead fans, over-stuffed furniture and a combination cook bartender.

Will Snyder Garcia in a poker game was equal to any gambler, unimpressed by grandeur or position. By midnight nobody else had had playable cards and the VP called it off. As Will was stuffing their money into his pockets the VP said, "Will, what do you want out of the railroad?"

Will looked around him. "My own business car."

"Maybe sooner than you think," the VP said. "Pack a bag and be here at eight in the morning."

In his room at the Montezuma Hotel, Will tossed and turned, wondering about his promotion and his own private car. Early, he was waiting, eager and ready, when the VP came down the steps of his.

"The President of Mexico," the VP said, "has agreed to reimburse the railroad for the damage done by the rebels. Now that the revolution has been put down and a quiet has settled, I need a smart, aggressive representative to see what the damage is. Although you need to be taught a thing or two about humility and diplomacy, you're the man. I have made arrangements for your business car."

They walked through Grand Avenue Gate, crossed the Line, and walked along a couple of private cars on a siding beside the Mexican customshouse, Will wondering which was to be his. When they got to the rear of the second car the VP said, "Not quite as luxurious as mine, but it will do the job because it will have to be carried across some rivers."

Will put on his poker face, shook hands with the VP and climbed aboard the handcar. As he went pumping south, coattails flying in the breeze of his own making, he was wondering if in some vague way he had just had a lesson in humility.

It turned out to be not such a bad deal after all. As a kind of dignitary on the railroad that was the lifeline for the villages down

the West Coast of Mexico he got free meals, free mescal, free lodging, and just enough free love to keep him satisfied.

His MO was: whenever he came to a bridge that had been damaged he went to the closest village and got the *alcalde* to sign a document attesting that the bridge had indeed been damaged and by whom.

Will was enjoying his sojourn when he arrived at a trestle near the Sinaloa-Nayarit border that had been blown up. This had been in El Colorado territory, El Colorado being famous for proficiency in wrecking trains and then going among the dead and dying plucking wallets from still-warm pockets, chopping off fingers to get at rings, knocking out teeth for the gold in them.

At the village nearby the entire population seemed to be crowded into the dirt-flooded cantina. There were mariachis and singing and lots of noise that quieted as Will strode up to the bar.

Conscious of every eye upon him, he asked the cantinero where he could find the alcalde.

"I am he," said the cantinero.

Will brought out his damage report and explained what it was, and that the railroad was to be reimbursed for the carnage and a bridge would be rebuilt, bringing work to the locals.

At the question as to who had done the damage, the cantinero-alcalde shouted, "El Colorado blew it up."

A huge, shirtless man with wild red hair spilling from under his white *sombrero*, lumpy with muscle, stood up slowly, towering menacingly higher and higher until his hat struck the *petate* ceiling, knocking down dust and scorpions. Long arms dangling, shoulders swinging, he roared in words considerably stronger than the following: "Who is this *gringo* that is looking for me?"

Villagers trooped ominously around Will, whose running muscles seemed suddenly paralyzed. He cried out: "So glad to meet you, *Senor* Colorado, valiant hero of the revolution, strong man of the people, I want to buy you a drink. To buy all a drink."

He showered money on the bar and the mob surged forward to get a share of the flowing mescal, leaving the way clear to the door. Then Will's muscles froze again when El Colorado shouted: "Wait!"

"Gotta move on down the road," Will said, hoping he sounded more like a busy executive than an humble auditor traveling on humble wheels.

"Wait," bellowed El Colorado, and turned his roar on the bartender. "Does it say who will pay for the bridge?"

"El Presidente,' the bartender said, and the room rocked with laughter.

"Sign it and let the man be on his way," El Colorado shouted above the noise. *"Viva el presidente."*

As Will walked jauntily back to his "business car" with the paper tucked safely into his pocket he wondered if he might also have just learned a lesson in hair-trigger diplomacy.

Shootout at Naco

Like more than half the people born on the border, Will Snyder carried his mother's maiden name, Garcia, tacked on to his father's. He was pushing 40, prematurely white-headed, dark-skinned, and looked very distinguished.

Railroad business had to go on in spite of the '29 revolution. Already no stranger to the damage civil war could cause, he was sent to Naco, Sonora, to audit the books of Huero Rendon, the SP de M agent there. Discrepancies in some of his reports had led to a belief he was possibly collaborating with one side or the other.

Dawn was just opening up the world for the day when Will dropped off a fast freight he had caught in Tucson. The first man he saw was Jose Garcia, a round fellow with squinty eyes and the only one with a Mexican surname among Arizona's Customs finest. He was some kind of relative of Will's. He was tilted in a chair against the wall of the U.S. customshouse, in civilian clothes, with a badge pinned to his shirt. The shirt was a veteran of many good meals.

After the big *abrazo* Joe wanted to know what Will was doing in his town. When Will told him, all Jose said was, "Poor Huero. He's got nothing but trouble."

Will trotted across the Line to the railroad depot. There was sporadic firing, a few singing ricochets, but nothing an agile man could not dodge.

He looked through a dusty pane of glass in the locked door of the agent's office. Huero was at his desk and just shook his head until Will held up his ID. Huero got up to look at it and let Will in.

"Guess I expected you," he said.

He looked much older than he was, and as if he had not slept for a month. The bags under his eyes were so heavy they pulled down the lids to expose their red rims. The office smelled like a barroom.

Huero's books were on the desk and an old Starr double-action .44 revolver was beside them. Will sat down and rolled up his sleeves, suggesting Huero go out for breakfast, but Huero said he had all he needed for nourishment right there, and sat down in a rickety chair with the bottle of mescal and stared at the floor. He was quiet except for the noise he occasionally made as he tilted the bottle.

Will worked right through, finishing just at dark.

"Well," Huero said, "you think they'll fire me when they read your report?"

"It's a possibility," Will admitted.

Huero came out and stood swaying on the station platform to watch Will run dodging through the bullets that were now flying around thicker than before.

Will felt safer inside the thick walls of the U.S. customhouse. Jose Garcia took him into the back room and stuffed him with beef, beans, and tortillas, talking above the sound of shots across the Line.

"Knowed Huero a long time, cousin," Jose said. "He has a wife that is prettier than a woman has a right to be. SP de M sent him off somewhere a while back. They've got a daughter in school so the wife stayed here and when Huero came back some neighbors told him she had been entertaining some other man which may or may not have been true. He's been on the bottle ever since."

"Sounds like he has real problems," Will said, thinking about that old revolver lying beside Huero's books.

He heard the distant whistle of the freight he was going to ride on up to Tucson, and stood up.

Jose said, "I hear all you railroaders are Masons. Isn't one of the principles to love your brother Mason?"

"Another one is truth," Will said, and stepped into the night. "Also prudence, fortitude, patience, and justice."

There was a loud noise and something kicked him in the stomach, right where his meal had settled. A man made a blacker shadow in the dark and Will wrestled with him, heard the gun go off again, then passed out.

When he regained consciousness he was in the Copper Queen Hospital, sewed and bandaged up tight. He heard Huero Rendon was in another room with a bullet in his thigh they were taking out.

Will guessed they thought that as soon as he was able he would go hunting for Huero, or if he didn't, the Law would, because Huero vanished overnight. Will thought his relative Jose Garcia might have had something to do with that.

Will left auditing for conductoring, then retired. He was in Monterrey to attend the christening of the first child of one of his many unknown relatives because he had been named godfather — not for the first time. The night before the ceremony he dropped in on a Masonic meeting and who should be Worshipful Master but Huero Rendon, older, more lined of face, but recognizable.

After the meeting Will sidled up to him. Huero turned pale. "I heard you were dead," he said, then hugged him and began to treat him like he was the Most Worshipful Grand Master of the Grand Lodge of the Pacific at least, wanted to know what he was doing there, and grinned when Will told him, then asked Huero about himself.

"Well," Huero said, "the Company transferred me out of Naco and I still had a job, but I didn't know why until I saw a copy of the

report you sent in saying that the mistakes seemed to be honest ones but that a transfer from Naco would be good for me and the Company. I was really mixed up that night, I thought if I made it look like a stray bullet killed you, you wouldn't be able to send in a report. And now you and I are some kind of shirt tail relatives."

Will said, "How do you figure that?"

Huero laughed. "Our daughter's son will be christened Guillermo Snyder Garcia-Rendon tomorrow. You figure it out."

When Will Snyder did, he discovered he had acquired one more relative—by marriage.

Duty-Free Booze

The SP de M rapido from Mexico customarily pulled one or two Pullmans into Nogales, Mexico and as the cars were pushed north across the border, customs officers took declarations from passengers and collected duty if any was due.

Private cars were even better treated.

In SP wire traffic one day there was a communication for Will Snyder Garcia from the head office in San Franciso: "Roberta Marcos requests your personal attention. She arrives Nogales tomorrow. Expedite crossing and escort her to Mexico City and return."

Roberta Marcos was a frequent border crosser. She was an energetic lady in her high fifties, addicted to multiple martinis and rare roast beef. She looked like a healthy Iowa girl who would relish a romp in a pile of cornhusks at the rustle of a corn tassel in any easy breeze. Age had nothing to do with her platinum hair, nor had age detracted from a figure that had lit fires in several rich men's furnaces.

Their gratitude had provided her with a monetary base on which to build an empire, using her natural gifts of shrewdness, wit, and wisdom as the mortar to cement the blocks of stocks and bonds that contributed to her ever-increasing wealth.

With all that money available to her, like some well-to-do folks, she could be miserly. She hated to pay Customs duties on merchandise in her baggage.

"Uniformed robbers," she would say of the Inspectors. "They'll be waiting a long time to get a penny out of me for duty."

The Bullet, the steam locomotive that pulled the once-a-day combination coach and express car from Tucson to the border came in as usual on time the next day, tugging Roberta's private car behind it. She was accompanied by a maid, a cook, a case of dry gin and a bottle of dry vermouth. She carried a snappish French poodle and already had a load on.

She was glad to see Will but the poodle was not and nibbled at Will's ankles every time he sat down to visit. Otherwise the trip to Mexico City was so pleasant Will was ashamed to take his salary. When they got there he spotted the car on a quiet siding so he could get plenty of undisturbed rest while she went out on the town. When she returned after three days of that, Will got her car hooked up to the rapido and saw to the reloading of her baggage and enough groceries to get back to San Francisco.

Among the groceries were 57 bottles of various liquors. He

CSP

predicted, "That stuff will cost you a fortune when we cross the border at Nogales. Duty and internal revenue taxes are very high."

"Do you want to bet I don't pay a cent?" she asked.

Will, knowing her, declined to bet.

When they were at Empalme near Guaymas and a couple hundred miles from the border Roberta ordered: "When we get to Nogales and before we cross I want you to bring Doc Tileman to me. I may be coming down with some infectious disease I wouldn't want to import."

Then she shooed him, the maid, the cook out of the car and kept only her obnoxious poodle beside her for the rest of the way to Nogales. Will hoped the dog would catch whatever she had and succumb.

Doc Tileman's office was just across the border where he could get first crack at border-crossers with the *turistas.* He was a big shuffling man who carried a dead Mexican cigar in his mouth at all times, even when he operated. He boasted he had the only license to practice medicine on both sides of the Line.

He stayed with Roberta as the car was pulled across the border with the Pullmans. When Customs Inspectors had worked their way back to the private car they saw the lady in bed hugging a poodle while Doc Tileman was trying to get his stethoscope past its sharp teeth and under a bare breast.

The Inspectors apologized for the necessity to disturb them, made a quick examination, and departed. When Doc Tileman came out he said to Will, "Not a damn thing wrong with that woman. She wants you."

Will went in. Roberta, fully-clothed, was getting out of the bed. "Help me here," she said, and threw back the covers. "Grab that heavy mattress and set it off."

Between the mattress and the frame of the bed were the 57 bottles.

"Lumpiest mattress I ever had my back on," she grumbled as she helped him carry the bottles back to the pantry. "And you lost your bet."

"How much did I bet?" Will asked.

"Oh, well," she said, "If you're going to quibble forget it."

As Will left he thought he detected a grin on the poodle's face and wondered about it until later he noticed a wet spot on the cuff of his trousers.

Snyder on Poker

Don Porfirio Mendoza's *barberia* was almost as popular as the Concordia and nearly as close to the Line. Many Customs and Immigration inspectors, *tomateros*, male citizens of Nogales, could get a haircut there, tip the barber, and get their shoes shined all for a quarter. That was when the *peso* was worth 12½¢ and went a long, long way.

Obese Don Porfirio has been gone a long time, like the value of the peso, his heart weakened by the miles of capillaries hidden in the fat he accumulated from reclining all day and half the night in a barber chair after he retired. But Manny Gomez still holds forth on the first chair, some of his toes sacrificed to gangrene, somewhat the worse for the wear and tear of *la bola*, but still on what is left of his feet.

Attrition reduced the ranks of the shop's clients, the new wave of produce people preferring to get their hair styled and blow-dried at Phantastic Pam's or the Mane Place for $24 a sitting, the Inspectors finding other shops where the barbers weren't hung up on one old-fashioned cut, but there was still a sprinkling of the faithful to come in, mostly from force of habit, to talk about old times.

Will Snyder Garcia was one of these. He was the border challenge to the good Sisters who ran the geriatrics ward at Holy Cross, because most people who entered there left through the back way and never returned, but for Will it was a revolving door, his recovery rate unsurpassed.

White-headed and thin as a grape stake, he came in every day he was able to, to have his lantern-jaw clean-shaven because, as he said, he wanted to be ready when he heard the final bugle call on Gabriel's trumpet.

He using a hearing aid so he would hear it, but half the time it didn't work and the rest of the time squealed like an alerted smoke alarm. The dark serge suit he wore could have been the same he had on when he retired as a conductor on the SP de M when it still was.

On a May day while Don Porfirio still ran the shop from his barber chair on an elevated platform at the rear, Will walked in and Don Porfirio said, "Here comes the ultimate gambler. The only man to bet the railroad he would live longer than he worked for it and won."

Will was having a problem with his hearing aid. "I'm not sure what you said but I'm sure it was disrespectful." He eased himself into Manny's chair and said, "Did I hear someone say something about gambling?"

"The usual?" Manny asked into his ear.

"Do you have anything else to offer?" Will said. "What's this talk about gamblers?"

Manny said, "Used to be some good games going on the rapido when you were conductor, weren't there?" It was easier to get on the same track with Will than try to take a siding.

"Games I remember best are those we had on the way down the West Coast. There would be Judge Julio Cano Delgado from Hermosillo, with the white goatee and the pot belly kept a girl friend up on Hereford Drive in Nogales for 30 years, bought a duplex and kept her in it so he would always have a place to sleep and somebody to do it with when he came up here. That's a switch. It's the gringos had the second families in Mexico. Then there would be Mister Payne, the Scotchman with mining property near Ures, he kept his family over on Sonoita Street. There was old Doc Freitag used to carry a case of lenses into Mexico, carry them right into the towns, set up shop in the plaza and fit eyes. Next trip he would bring the glasses. And the thread salesman we called Turk, had the shop up on Arroyo where he kept his stock and filled his orders. And Manuel Avila, the cotton grower with the farms out on the road to Bahia Kino.

"I remember one day we started playing before we left Lomas headed south. I dealt *libre*. Mr. Payne passed three kings, hoping to rope in a sucker. The Judge opened for four-bits as any damn fool would. I looked down and found I held four queens so I called the four-bits and Mr. Payne hiked the pot seven dollars and a half, all it would stand, as a gentleman should. I called with my four queens, hoping Mr. Payne would help his hand, which he drew two cards. I asked for one. I checked, as a poker player should, and Mr. Payne dribbled out about $25 with seeming reluctance. So I hesitated, meowed, bellyached, and then called his $25 and raised just a nubbin. He took the hook and came back with $60 more. I called and hiked him $175. He laid down a king full with great glee and reached for the pot. I said, 'Take a gander at this,' and displayed my four lovely ladies. Mr. Payne burst into profuse perspiration and got so mad he left the train at Magdalena instead of Hermosillo. You can figure out the size of the pot. For the moment I was damned affluent for that day and age."

Manny said, "You wrote a book about gambling once, didn't you?"

"SNYDER ON POKER," Will said. "It was all blank pages except for the center fold and there on the pages in big capital letters it said: "*Bet all cinches freely.*"

In Pursuit of Idleness

Customs Inspector Tony Russo came to Nogales during WW I as an airplane mechanic for two temperamental Jenny's that were more on the ground than in the air. Waiting for spare parts. he was so often unoccupied he developed a taste for idleness.

When he married Julieta Rosas and was discharged from the Army both in the same week he wanted to lie around and think where he could get a job that paid as much for so little work. Julieta, who worked at the Ville de Paris, wasn't having any part of that.

Russo heard about them needing a hand at the Bar Lazy S. The "lazy" part sounded good to him. Furthermore, he had never seen a cowboy bust his *culo* at anything. All they did was ride around on horses and that suited Russo.

The rancher who owned the Bar Lazy S was Willie Brown, known for honesty and fairness. He looked like the male half of *American Gothic*.

"You don't know anything about handling stock," he said. "You'd have to start from the ground up."

"What's that mean?" Russo asked warily.

"Apprentice cowboy. Follow me."

Russo followed him to a big adobe barn, thinking maybe he was going to start to learn to ride a horse, which did not seem like any big deal.

Brown said, "You good at hoeing Texas weeds?"

"What do I know?" Russo said. "Only weeds that grew where I lived came up in the cracks of the pavement."

"You'll learn quick," Mr. Brown said. "Grab that axe."

He led Russo to a shallow wash choked with young mesquite trees with trunks as thick as a wrestler's wrist and said, "These weeds take up space we need for grass and they use too much water. Mow 'em down."

Russo was ready to quit before he got the job, but then he thought about his soft and tender bride and how disappointed she would be if he came home without work.

Blisters like balloons grew on his hands, his fingers cramped into aching hooks. The hot Friday sun burned down. Buzzards circled in the copper sky and Russo wondered if they were waiting for him to die of fatigue.

He had charley horses in his arms, shoulders and back before Mr. Brown showed up on the bank of the wash and said, "You done good. You can stop for now. Come back Sunday at sun-up."

Russo was grateful for a Saturday off. Julieta pricked his blisters

CSP

and put mutton tallow on his raw hands, rubbed his arms and shoulders and back with tequila when she came home from work. They also drank some and he felt so much better that they honeymooned most of the night.

But he was working a lot harder than he liked to. Fence-mending, screw-worm-doctoring, well-greasing, Russo was progressing up to horseback-riding the hard way.

On Friday night Mr. Brown paid him and Rodney Whitney, the journeyman permanent cowboy. Russo rode to Nogales with Whitney on the bus.

"What's with this old man Brown?" Russo asked. "Day's off Saturday, work on Sunday?"

Whitney said, "Seventh Day Adventists. No work from sundown Friday until sun-up on Sunday."

Russo began to think real hard about that.

When the next Friday came and Mr. Brown paid them and said he would see them Sunday at sun-up Russo said, "Mr. Brown, I wanted to talk to you about that. You observe your Sabbath on Saturday, Whitney and I are used to having ours on Sunday. Now we work, and that keeps us from worshipping as we should to keep us from sinful ways. You being known as a fair man, I thought maybe we could make a deal."

Mr. Brown said thoughtfully, "What do you have in mind?"

"Instead of us coming in on Sunday we could come in Monday at sun-up. That way you get your Sabbath, and we get ours."

The old man fingered his smooth-shaven chin. "You mean you would be off Saturday *and* Sunday? I'd have to talk to Mother about that. Your're willing to give up a day's pay and work harder to get everything done?"

Russo said sadly "Not really."

The old man proved his fairness when he agreed not only to give them their Sunday off, but to continue their pay as it was as long as they kept up their end of the work.

So it is generally conceded that Tony Russo, in his pursuit of idleness, was the one who introduced the five-day work-week long before it became the law of the land for government employees in the area.

Where's the Beef?

During World War II the Government of the United States sent a contingent of warriors into Mexico for another kind of battle. This was the continuing one against *aftosa* and there was a whole lot of killing, mostly of infected cattle, in order to stamp out what was considered a threat to the American beef business. The then Bureau of Animal Industry mounted a second line of defense, stationing men at border ports to assist the Customs Service, which was charged with the responsibility for stopping importations of fresh *carne de res* through the Gates, not even a soup bone or a spoonful of lard.

The restriction worked a real hardship on many poor folks, for although the meat was not Kansas City beef and tended to be tough and stringy, folks found that marinating it in ground dry papaya made it chewable, and it cost a lot less than meat at Puchi's or the Safeway. Meat smuggling was inevitable.

Customs Inspectors carried guns but the BAI men were unarmed until Rodney Whitney, the ex-cowboy now working for BAI as a border guard, and Orval Winterbotham, prominent international lawyer, teamed up and got them sharp knives.

Rodney Whitney still wore his regulation cowboy uniform of faded blue shirt, faded Levis, dusty boots, wide-brimmed Stetson, and a sack of Bull Durham in his left shirt pocket with the tag hanging out.

Tony Russo and Whitney were friends from the Bar Lazy S days, so Whitney would sit cross-legged on a baggage inspection bench behind Russo while Russo worked traffic.

Russo believed that neither his salary nor his standing in the community depended upon the number of seizures he made and rarely made one. So it was noticeable when he suddenly began making more meat seizures than all the other Customs Inspectors combined. Russo enjoyed his notoriety.

Unwilling to kick a gift horse in the mouth, Russo never asked Whitney how he was able to distinguish with such certainty those who were smuggling fresh cuts of beef from those who weren't. But there was a struggle within him when Belle Winterbotham, the overweight wife of the border's leading attorney, who could afford the best of anything, crossed the border from Mexico and Whitney said quietly from behind him, "Mrs. Winterbotham has meat."

Whitney had never been wrong yet, so finally Russo asked, "Belle, you bringing any meat today?"

"Why, Tony," she replied indignantly, "not today, not any day."

"In that case," he said, "you won't mind stepping out while I look."

Belle's round red face turned ashen. She stammered, hesitated, finally backed out of the car, trying to block Russo's view with her ample bottom, but he saw her knock a package she had been sitting on under the seat.

He gave her the alternative of taking the fresh beef roast back to Mexico or he would seize it.

"I don't want anything more to do with it, Tony," she said. "I'm so embarrassed. Please don't tell anyone."

Russo did not smile. "Tell you what, Belle. It will be our secret if you promise never to bring any fresh meat again."

"Where's the Bible?" she raised her right hand. "I do most solemnly and sincerely swear."

So Tony called a Mexican celador over and gave him the meat which made him happy, prevented entry of the beef into the U.S., and took Belle Winterbotham off the seizure report. It was called border diplomacy.

But eventually Belle got to thinking she had been wronged and told her husband, Orval, about the incident.

That specialist in international law had been a leading Nogales citizen for so long he wore his tenure like a purple mantle of royalty. He knew Tony's action was within his authority but as a descendant of a pioneer family he felt bound to protest.

Russo slyly referred him to Rodney Whitney.

Whitney listened courteously while Orval, with lawyer logic said, "Beef can be infested with aftosa bugs, but after it is brought across the Line, refrigerated until cooked at 450 degrees for three hours, then is eaten, then evacuated, then along with other effluent floats to the sewage disposal plant at the north edge of town where it is further broken down into liquids so pure they say you can drink it, how many bugs would still be alive and active?"

Whitney said, "I see your point. I have a suggestion that a citizen of your stature could make to your legislative representatives and be listened to: how would it be if people were allowed to bring meat already cooked across the Line?"

Winterbotham's personal grievance was lost in his delight at finding a possible loophole in a law and he took the matter up with his Senator. Soon a directive came down: along with a couple of butcher knives per port, that cooked beef could cross as long as it was sliced into and found to be well-done and not rare.

This slowed but did not stop entirely the smuggling of fresh beef. Tony Russo continued to make seizures, relying on Whitney's incredible intuition.

A day came, though, when Whitney did not show up, and Tony

made no seizures. Later Russo telephoned him, saying: "A little Mexican kid will come by asking you for a quarter and piece of chalk. Give it to him, I won't be back for a few days. I have been paying him to watch the butcher shop across the Line and make a chalk mark on the left front tire on the cars of gringos who come out with packages and I think we should keep him on the payroll."

White Gold

Dutch Herold was tall, thin, with brown hair streaked with grey. Twin red spots rode high on his cheeks under steady brown eyes. He did not look much like a hero, but two days after Collector Cornell put him temporarily on the Gates at Nogales awaiting an opening in the Mounted Patrol, he became one.

He was seated in a chair, propped against the wall of the International Bank at Morley Avenue, dozing and dreaming he was back in the Philippines with the Army, skinning mules, when a fusillade of gunfire broke out. A bullet struck the adobe wall behind him, showered him with dirt, and sung off across Morley on a dying note.

Dutch did not excite easily, so he opened his eyes lazily in time to see a small American with pumping arms and reaching legs running head down out of Mexico, closely pursued by an irate Mexican cutting down on him at every jump with a huge revolver.

Dutch customarily moved with the casual agility of a desert tortoise and saw no need to change his habit now. As the gringo scampered past, Dutch stood up, squared his hat, and stepped into the path of the running gunman who immediately applied the brakes and skidded to a dusty stop, his revolver barrel touching Dutch's heart.

Dutch moved his hand up, deflected the barrel, and took the weapon from the man's hand. Several witnesses saw the action. Before long, the Collector strolled up to compliment Dutch on enhancing the reputation of the Outside Force as men difficult to intimidate.

Dutch told him, "Collector Cornell, I am not very good at arithmetic, but I can count to six. That man's gun was empty when I took it away from him."

"That," the Collector said, "will be our secret."

Dutch Herold took a liking to Shorty Newman, one of the Mounted Patrolmen. One day Shorty needed two dollars and asked Dutch for a loan. Before he could pay it back a new station was established and Dutch was transferred out there as the Patrolman.

It was at a place called Gunsight, near what today is Why. It was so isolated, situated there between the new Cornelia mines and the International Line near Mexican Sonoyta that the Collector's political conscience began to trouble him and he had afterthoughts, particularly as the former mule-skinner had come to the Customs Service well-recommended by the Provisional Governor of the Philippines, William Howard Taft, now President of the U.S. Still,

he did not believe he could uproot a settled verteran Mounted Inspector to send him out there in exchange for Dutch without causing a measure of discontent among his troops so he did what he thought was the next best thing. He gave Dutch a brand new Dodge automobile to increase his mobility.

He summoned Shorty Newman, who was a good mechanic and driver and said, "Look, we've just got our first machine for the Patrol. Take it out to Dutch Herold and stay with him until you teach him to drive."

Shorty had thrown his bedroll into the Dodge when he

remembered the two dollars he owed Dutch. He didn't have that much cash in his pocket, neither did his wife, so he told her to write out a check for Dutch Herold. It was late when he arrived at Gunsight and he did not think about the check until the next morning.

Dutch studied it carefully, then said, "Mr. Newman, don't you have two dollars?"

"No," Shorty replied.

Dutch handed the check back and said in his slow way, "Then I wish you would take this back to Mrs. Newman. She don't owe me nothin'."

He was not quick to learn how to drive the machine, but Newman was finally satisfied he would be able to follow the ruts to Ajo for supplies and left him.

The first time Dutch drove to Ajo alone he was halfway there when a sassy coyote stepped into the road, sat down on his haunches, and lolled his tongue out at Dutch.

Dutch slammed on the brakes, unslung his revolver, and got that insolent animal with one shot between the eyes — right through the windshield.

He put the Dodge car behind his shack and let it gather dust. His two mules were all the transportation he needed to patrol, and he was doing just that some years and a few Collectors later in a place he, and probably nobody else, had been before, cutting sign when he noticed he was riding over some white stuff. He dismounted, scooped up a sample of it, and as an afterthought, laboriously wrote some claim notices on some cigarette papers and staked the place out.

Next time he was in Ajo he got the assayer at the new Cornelia mines to run some tests on it. It turned out to be a material much needed as a flux in their smelting process that was now being shipped in at great cost and inconvenience from the Mojave Desert.

Dutch Herold would have been the first to admit he was not the smartest man in the Mounted Patrol, but when he took his retirement shortly after, he was the richest.

Security Test

Sheriff Godofredo Garcia was distantly related to Will Snyder Garcia and to Graciela Garcia. He was nowhere near as attractive as she, having a flabby figure, ears distinctively elephantine, a bulbous nose, pink jowls, and a naivete unscarred by much contact with the world outside of Santa Cruz County.

On a Monday morning he drove to the police station in the City Hall under the clock tower and picked up his cousin, Ernie Garcia. Ernie was tall, thin, and narrow of face. People nicknamed him Cara Caballo.

It was the custom of these two lawmen to exchange information of any rare violations of law in their respective jurisdictions during the night before, over a cup of coffee at Little Jimmy's Border Cafe on Morley Avenue next to Leap Cornell's International Bank, on the corner diagonally across from the Morley Avenue garita.

The sheriff carefully steered the old Nash into Park Street, passed the north end of the stone depot, bounced across the railroad tracks and down the alley that ran behind the Morley Avenue stores. As was their usual routine he parked the car behind the bank.

A dusty red Chevrolet touring car was parked where they usually stopped, and Chief Garcia grumbled, "If I wasn't in such a hurry to get some of Little Jimmy's slop he calls coffee down me I'd stick a ticket under the wiper."

The two lawmen grunted their way out of the car and walked along International Avenue around the back to the Border Cafe. They lingered over their coffee until the publisher of the daily paper and no friend of the bureaucracies came in for his, wondering aloud if crime stopped while the top law officers were sipping theirs.

Crime along the Line in those days was limited. Nearly every other person was an enforcement officer of some kind, with the visible symbol of his authority hanging from his belt. Even though it was only a step to Mexico and sanctuary, would-be robbers didn't have the courage to run the gauntlet of border guards.

As they re-passed the bank's window, Chief Garcia glanced in. Although his view was partly obscured by reflections there were folks already lined up at the counter making deposits even though it was not yet ten.

"I see Herb Sloan isn't losing any time picking up the Mexican pesos collected over the weekend across the Line," he remarked.

"Easier to handle that curio store, cantina, and cathouse cash early than during regular business hours?" Sheriff Garcia suggested.

They gave casual acknowledgement to the waves of the Inspectors

on duty at the Gate, who were seated on high swivel stools they had dragged halfway into International Avenue in order to get the morning sun.

The Garcias had opened doors on the Nash and were preparing to step in when the bank's back door banged back and a skinny man hurried out. He wore a dirty grey Stetson, a blue denim work shirt, wrinkled Levis worn off at the bottom from being too long, and a handerchief mask. In one hand he held a large canvas bank money bag, in the other was a large revolver.

Sheriff Garcia drew his sidearm.

Chief Garcia drew his.

The man clumping down the steps in worn over high-heeled boots yelled, "Don't shoot, for Christ's sake. Didn't Herb Sloan tell you about this bank security test?"

He tossed mask, revolver, canvas sack into the front seat of the red Chevy and went in after them complaining: "Somebody could get killed—" then his voice blended into the sound of his starting engine.

Not looking at each other, the two lawmen holstered their weapons. The red Chevrolet drew slowly away, making a quick right to climb over the railroad tracks, past the south end of the depot toward the Grand Avenue Gate a half-block away.

The bank's door banged open again, Cashier Herb Sloan, face the color of putty, staggered out. His yellow hair was disarrayed and blood trickled from a huge lump on his forehead.

He jabbed a forefinger toward the Grand Avenue Gate and shouted, "He just stole all the pesos I had in the bank."

He and the Garcias watched the red Chevrolet creep past the celadores under the canopy of their garita and disappear into Nogales, Sonora, Mexico.

Chief Garcia shook his head mournfully and said loudly, "Looks like we got here a tad too late."

"A minute earlier," Sheriff Garcia said even more loudly, "we would have stopped him cold."

Whatever Became of Luke Short?

On May 18, 1914 the Collector of Customs at Nogales received an informative telegram from his deputy at Douglas: "Luke Short shot and killed a Mexican here tonight."

Aficionados of Western lore will recognize the name Luke Short: five foot six, 140 pounds, profession: gambler, contemporary of Wyatt Earp, Doc Holliday, Bat Masterson and other veterans of Tombstone, Dodge City, Leadville. He shot a few men and became top gun of uptown gambling in Fort Worth until his death from dropsy—then a euphemism for alcoholism—at the age of 39.

Mounted Inspector of Customs Luke Short was not that man, although efforts have been made to link them. A few things mesh: both were from Texas, both were in Pima County in Arizona, but Inspector Short was only 19 when the gambling Short died.

Inspector Short worked on the side of the law, first as a County Mountie, then as an Arizona State Ranger, then a Constable, and a Pima County Deputy Sheriff, arriving well-recommended to Customs in 1912. He was an exemplary citizen until the incident mentioned in the telegram quoted above, and even in that he was merely complying with the Code of the West.

The killing was not performed in the line of duty, but was the result of an insult to Short's wife by one Eduardo Soto. When Short learned about it he let it be known that the next time he saw Soto he planned to do him no good.

Soto got the message and for a few days stayed out of Short's sight, but Douglas was small, life had to go on, and eventually the two met.

Soto was on a wagon, accompanied by one Pompeo Villagrana. They were at the corner of 11th Street and F Avenue when Short, mounted, came loping up the street behind them, his horse kicking up little puffs of dust as the animal carried its rider into his and Soto's immediate and uncertain future.

In an effort to settle his quickly, Soto reached into the bib of his overalls and pulled out a gun when Short was about twenty feet from the wagon. Short drew his and the firefight was on.

Short kept coming, much to the dismay of Villagrana, who suddenly found himself between Soto and Short with bullets big as bumble bees buzzing around his ears amid deafening gunfire. He would have made an excellent eyewitness except that he was much too busy trying to dodge flying lead to take much notice of what was happening.

Ten shots were fired in five seconds. Only one of Soto's took

CSP

effect. It struck Short's horse in the right hind leg.

The scene could have been right out of the heart of any Western movie: Short trying to wrestle his rearing horse into a position where he could return Soto's fire, the sudden cloud of yellow dust lifted by the hoofs of Short's horse and Soto's panicked animals plunging in their traces, Soto's head appearing abruptly above the dust cloud as two of Short's bullets struck him in the chest, jerked him upright, pitched him crashing down to the street. Then him struggling to get on his feet, and staggering into Wamel's store.

Short's two bullets did terminal damage, for Soto died within an hour. Short gave himself up to the Deputy Sheriff and was held under bond until a coroner's jury found he had acted in self-defense.

One might wonder if the verdict would have been the same had Soto been the victor. After all, Short had made a threat to do him bodily injury on sight, so the question of who drew first was not particularly relevant.

Things kind of sloped downhill for Short from that point on, but nothing dramatic happened for a year and a half, at which time he got into another duel, this time it was his gun against a waiter's catsup bottle. Short came out the loser, was charged with assault with a deadly weapon in superior court and got a 30-day suspension without pay from Customs.

Customs, ever loyal to one of its own, cut a deal with the County Attorney whereby if Short was transferred out of the county, the charges, which carried a mandatory sentence of a year in jail, would be dropped. But other Districts would not cooperate, for his recent reputation preceded him everywhere and nobody would take him.

Erratic behavior had become such a way of life for him that it had attracted the attention of the police. He was of those who should never take a drink, for even a single shot seemed to affect his judgement and make him quarrelsome.

On a bright May morning he got into an argument with his horse in front of the Customhouse, unlimbered that ever ready revolver, and fired at its feet. Ricochets sang through the walls of the outhouse where a Clerk/Inspector was seated, reading the *Douglas Dispatch.*

He survived the incident, but Short did not, for within 30 days he was dismissed from the Service.

Some 33 years later the Immigration and Naturalization Service tried to determine Short's citizenship for the purpose of establishing that of a lady who said she was married to him from about 1914 to 1924. The information requested from Customs records was to include the date of his death, but as far as Customs was concerned, Luke Short was terminated at the close of business on July 31, 1916 and was never heard from again.

False Bottoms

Billy Cardwell, the bright young Customs Inspector, and Al Martin, Immigration, had the graveyard shift at Grand Avenue on a rainy night in August. The midnight traffic flurry had passed, they had both walked inside the garita where big Al griped while Eddie alphabetized the day's declarations that now there was nothing to do until the six o'clock exodus of local crosser-workers from Mexico.

"Don't expect me to do your work for you while you play solitaire with those cards," Martin said, just as a carload of soldiers from Fort Huachuca pulled into the traffic lane.

Cardwell got up and walked out. The GIs were loudly, profanely inebriated but Cardwell's instincts told him there was something phony about their jollity, so he suggested that they disembark so he could look around.

The three in the front seat did so quickly, but those in the back were aggressively reluctant.

"Hell, man," one said, "we didn't bring nothing from Mexico except maybe a venereal disease."

Then everybody but Cardwell roared with hilarious laughter. He might have, too, if he hadn't heard it 1000 times before.

When they finally stepped down they left behind a small, mud-streaked young woman on whom they had planted their heavy wet muddy boots in order to hide her from casual scrutiny.

"Just bringing something home for the boys in the barracks," one said, which broke the rest of them up again until huge Al Martin strolled out to take charge of the illegal entrant, a prostitute from Canal Street, and Cardwell continued his search, directing the driver to open the car's trunk, in which he found a large cardboard carton full of photographs.

"I'm Post photographer," the driver explained. "I forgot those were in there."

The photos were clearly designed to appeal to the prurient, and because there were many copies of some of them, they were as clearly designed to be sold. Cardwell seized them under the same statute that exists today but is rarely enforced.

After Martin had sent the girl back to Mexico, after Cardwell had gotten names and addresses to pass on to the Provost Marshal at the Post, the sobered GIs left. Martin and Cardwell settled down to pass the time inventorying and examining the pictures to be sure they were, indeed, pornographic.

They were thus absorbed in their work when a small Mexican boy walked out of Mexico carrying a jug of Bacardi rum and declared it.

He was almost immediately followed by a grinning gringo who hung around outside the garita, looking in.

The boy had no documents and readily stated that the man was to give him a dollar to bring the jug across. Cardwell invited the man inside.

"You promised this boy a dollar to bring this jug?" he asked.

"Yes," the man said.

"Then give it to him."

The man confessed that as this was his second importation within 30 days he hadn't been entitled to bring it free of duty and so had hired the kid. Al Martin made his second voluntary departure that night when he sent the boy back to Mexico where he belonged.

"All right," Cardwell said to the violator, "we'll make it easy on you. Pay the duty and Internal Revenue tax and you can take it with you."

The man said he had given the boy his last dollar. Cardwell searched him and found nothing but a bus ticket and a set of false teeth.

"My bottoms," the man said. "I don't use 'em much."

It was unprecedented, but Cardwell said he would just hold the teeth until the man brought the money in, which he promised to do at 8 a.m. and gave as his address the El Dorado Inn in Tucson, where he was a waiter.

As he didn't show up at the appointed hour, Cardwell explained to the Chief how there happened to be an undocumented gallon of rum on hand. The Chief nearly choked on his laughter, saying that was probably one of the funniest things that had ever happened on the Line.

Cardwell went home and to bed. At 9 Maureen awakened him. "Chief's on the phone. Sounds grim."

"That man hasn't appeared," the Chief said, "and the Collector says for you to get up to Tucson fast and give him back his teeth before he starves to death and sues the government."

In Tucson, Cardwell learned the man quit early that morning and jumped a bus for L.A. Billy Cardwell was stuck with a set of lowers he didn't need, an uncollectible bill, and a tale that would haunt him the rest of his days with Customs. He drove back to Nogales and stopped at Saldamando's drug store for a Coke at their soda fountain before going home to continue his interrupted sleep.

Big Al Martin was guzzling down a double chocolate malt in a very tall glass through two straws. Cardwell sat beside him and Martin said, "I not only have to work with you all night I have to suffer your presence all day, too?" He turned away to admire a pretty

lady stepping out the door into brilliant sunlight. She wore a thin cotton dress.

Cardwell picked up Al's check and said, "Well, let me buy."

Martin said, "I take back anything mean I might have said."

"And anything mean you might say in the future?"

"Well—"

Cardwell walked out on Martin's pause. He heard later that goods shook off the shelves and a window display caved in at the roar Martin let out when he sucked the last of his chocolate malt up the two straws and found a set of false lower teeth staring up at him from the bottom of the glass.

The $25 Insult

It takes all kinds.

Elmo Greene on the Line was one of a kind, Dan Shea of another. Elmer was a practicing Baptist, Dan a fallen Catholic.

Elmo was not so much big as he was wide. Kids, friends of his kids, who had been in his house, said there was a specially-made pillow on his bed to accommodate the distance from his head to the point of his shoulder whenever he slept on his side. They said it was full of cornshucks. Elmo was from Iowa.

Dan Shea was stout, too, and whatever he lacked in big he made up for in bluster. He had no kids. He was very unpopular not only with his co-workers, but the border crossers as well. His complaint file was thicker than anybody else's.

It was a practice, on cold winter days or nights, to take turns working traffic. Those not working would go into the one-man shelter booth between lanes to thaw out in front of the small electric heater. Sometimes it would get so crowed, so stuffy and hot in there, it was hard to breathe.

If little Jimmy Gleason was one of those and it got too crowded, he had a unique method of clearing it of everyone but himself — he would surreptitiously break wind.

When only two Inspectors were on duty, the one not working could warm up in the booth and while away his 20 minutes off by reading comics, the sports page in *The Arizona Daily Star* or, in Elmo Greene's case, the Good Book.

Dan Shea thought of Elmo as a fat, Bible-thumping idiot and delighted in disturbing Elmo's rest period by kicking on the narrow wooden door or rattling keys against the window pane. Elmo would simply smile and turn the other cheek.

One bitter, breath-steaming Monday morning they were working together. Shea was nursing a hangover developed over the weekend, checking traffic. Greene was in the shelter booth reading his Bible.

This was before auto manufacturers began making many different models and putting different names on each one. The car that drove into the traffic lane was a simple blue Dodge coupe, the one with the trunk compartment large enough to accommodate a horse.

The driver was a big cowboy who had been across the Line drinking tequila and wearing himself out on the girls in Canal Street since Friday night. His name was Randy Ayers and he slanted a bloodshot look up at Dan Shea when Shea said, "Where were you born?"

Ayers replied, "Drop dead."

Shea didn't like that at all but was able to accept it as a declaration of American citizenship on the ground that nobody but an American would pick such a time and place to make such a stupid remark. Aside from that, it was immigration business and Shea, being a Customs Inspector, couldn't have cared less.

However, he did feel a need to demonstrate his authority, so he said, "What are you bringing from Mexico?"

Ayers grunted, "Nothing but a headache and a droopy—"

Shea interrupted. "Open the trunk anyway."

Ayers took the keys from the ignition and held them out. "You want to look in the trunk, you open it."

Shea said "Get your ass out here and open it yourself."

When Ayers got out and stood up, with his tall grey Stetson and high-heeled boots, he was seven feet high. He clumped around to the back of the car and flung up the lid on its vast emptiness.

"Next time," Shea said, "spare me all that lip."

Ayers slammed down the lid. "Just because you sons of bitches—" he began, but was interrupted by a sudden mouthful of Shea's knuckles.

Ayers was so enraged by Shea's rudeness that he knocked him down and raised a foot to give him the boot and keep him down.

Elmo Greene closed his Bible and came out of the shelter booth so fast his broad shoulders brought part of the door frame with him. He barrelled into Ayers, bear-hugged him around the waist, lifted him off his feet, ran him into the garita and slammed him against the back wall so hard all the fight went out of him. It startled the shift Captain so much he dropped his coffee cup and broke it.

Shea wanted to make a big Federal case out of it called assaulting a Federal officer in the performance of his duty, but wiser heads prevailed seeing as he had struck the first blow. He did insist, though, in bringing Ayers before the city magistrate on a charge of disturbing the peace at the Grand Avenue Gate. Ayers was fined $25 and sent on his way.

That didn't satisfy Shea. He argued that the penalty should have been greater, firmly believed he was justified in hitting Ayers in the mouth after he and his fellow officers had been grossly slandered.

Judge Tiburcio Moreno, who had known Shea since they were both boys and never did like him, didn't see it that way at all.

He said, "You people down there on the Line are paid well-enough you can afford a $25 insult now and then."

It was really poor Elmo Greene got the dirty end of the stick. It wasn't in Shea's nature to be grateful to him for saving him from broken facial bones and a kicked-in rib cage, so Elmo got no thanks from him, and had to help repair the broken door frame, too.

Pioneer Woman

No Customs port on the border of Arizona with Sonora has been as shifty as Sasabe, where a port of entry was created by the road up from Puerto Libertad, but it settled down in its present location in 1916. The Customs and Immigration officers then lived and worked out of three tents, but by the time Sid and May Hansen arrived on the scene 25 years later, the town had a stable population of 50 and a six-year old Customs House. There had been more houses on the block they lived in in San Francisco than there were in the sprawling townsite.

It was dark when they got there, having driven straight through in a car as overloaded as any Grapes of Wrath transportation, down a dirt road that seemed to have no end. The wind was blowing, dust gritted between their teeth.

May put a sheet down on a lumpy couch and laid her new baby on that while she went to help Sid and a nice neighbor lady, wife of an Immigration officer, unload. When she came back into the house with a couple of suitcases she saw an ugly black, brown, red and white creature ten inches long with a hundred legs crawling down the back of the couch toward her baby.

She snatched up the child and ran out screaming. Jane, who had been in Sasabe for a year and qualified as an old timer, walked over to the couch and ran her hand down between the seat and the back and brought up the wriggling centipede.

When she carried it outside and stomped it to death she said, "You'll get used to these and other crawly things." But May wasn't so certain her marriage would last that long.

Sid had to report for duty at the Port at midnight, newcomers always getting the graveyard shift, so May had to iron a shirt so he would present a proper appearance to the handful of Papago Indians and the two or three regulars who would come stumbling out of darkest Mexico. She laid some towels on the table and started the pressing job.

The lights went out. Nobody had told her that the town's electricity was furnished by a generator that was turned off whenever the town's enterprising owner was ready for bed.

Again Jane to the rescue with a sad iron, the kind you put on top of the wood stove and heat, removing it with a detachable handle when it was hot enough. May managed to drop it and break it, thus earning the enmity of the other wives in town who depended on it, but not before she had ironed cuffs, collar, and front of the shirt and burned her hands in a dozen places.

In the morning after having done a washing by hand and hung it out to dry, she was sitting in the yard in the only chair they had been furnished that wasn't crippled. The baby was on a blanket taking the sun as Sid slept after coming off the graveyard shift and telling her his experiences: "There I was, sitting in front of the Customhouse, trying to stay awake when I heard this horse coming out of Mexico. Into the light comes a big Indian on a white horse. Behind the horse walks this Indian lady, her arms full of packages of groceries. I said to the big Indian, 'Shouldn't your wife be riding?' which seemed to me to be the only fair way. He turned around to look at her. In a minute he said, 'she doesn't have a horse,' like any idiot should have known that."

Mary was less than certain, now that the test had come, that she would follow Sid to the ends of the Earth.

She was reading a week-old newspaper when she heard the

raucous sound of a disturbed roadrunner that was dancing on top of the ocotillo fence that surrounded their yard, looking down at a three-foot rattlesnake on a direct path to investigate the squirming bundle of warm baby.

Sid's .38 Colt issue revolver in its holster hung from its belt from the back of the chair she was sitting in. She had never had a gun in her hand, but she snatched the weapon, squeezed off a shot with her eyes closed, decapitated the surprised rattler and sent the roadrunner screeching off in a low, excited trajectory.

She gradually became accustomed to hardships pioneer women had to endure. She welcomed the early spring, for winter in Sasabe can be hideous. She was on her knees, pulling weeds from her small vegetable garden with the baby cooing on her blanket when something moved before May's hands. She snatched them back as a miniature prehistoric monster looked out at her with predatory beady eyes.

Sid was gone with his revolver but there was a double-barrelled bird-shooting shotgun, a 12-gauge, leaning against the wall just inside the door. She reached for it, lifted it, pointed it, closed her eyes, pulled both triggers, knocked herself back against the wall of the house.

She missed the Gila monster completely and had a sore arm and shoulder for a week, but the muzzle blast cleaned out the garden, weeds and all, so she didn't need to do any hoeing. Neither, for that matter, did she have any fresh vegetable that season.

Sasabe had had a few break-ins and robberies. Nobody had yet been hurt but Sid bought a 9 mm Colt Commander anyway, for May's protection when he was away at the Port, which was just out of scream range. She slept with it under her pillow, and just the feel of its hard outline under her head gave her a feeling of security. One morning when she was making the bed the thing went off and filled the room with feathers from her pillow.

Although Naco, east along the border, was scarcely a thriving metropolis, at least there was a deputy sheriff in Bisbee just a few miles away, so when they were transferred there a few months later, at last May felt she was back under big city police protection.

Hide-out Gun

The entire border community was shocked and saddened when somebody got into Marie Windsor's place in Rancho Grande Estates near Nogales. She must have walked in while the house was being ransacked. Marie was an ex-school teacher, 88 years old, never had harmed anybody in her whole life, but she was killed in an extra-ordinarily cruel way.

They arrested Juan Gomez, a former pupil, and Superior Court Judge Alberto Monroy sent him up to the prison in Florence forever. As they dragged Gomez out of the courtroom, he was screaming how he would break out and come back and kill the rest of those who had persecuted him all his life.

Ed Wilson was one of those, if you wanted to look at it Gomez' way. As Customs officer, Wilson shook Gomez down every time he crossed the Line on Wilson's shift. Intuition and persistence paid off when Ed arrested Gomez for smuggling narcotics and put him behind the bars for two years.

"If I had paid attention to all the threats on my life I had during 32 years of law enforcement," the retired Customs officer said, "I would have worried myself into the Greenhouse years ago."

Just the same, when he was informed of Gomez' escape, he took his .38 Colt Cobra from its secret hiding place in the headboard of their bed, cleaned it, put fresh loads in it, and put it back in its accustomed nest.

That afternoon Junior, Shelly, his wife, and their three-year-old son, Third, drove down from Tucson for a Sunday visit.

They didn't call Ed Wilson, Jr., Junior on his job with the Tucson PD, they called him Captain. One wall of his office was covered with medals he had won for marksmanship. Ed took partial credit for those because Junior's early training in guns came from him. He had also taught Junior to give weapons their due respect, which was why they were both alarmed when Third worked open the sliding patio door and toddled out of the bedroom staggering under the weight of Ed's Cobra held tightly in his tiny hands.

Big Junior moved the fastest. He took the weapon from Third's grasp and unloaded it, holding it indecisively for a moment.

Ed read his son's thoughts. "Give it back to him. You cut your teeth on my gun barrel."

Junior shook his head slowly. "And it was always loaded because you were afraid of the unloaded kind. So I was lucky, and so were my friends. Where do you keep this?"

Ed showed him. "How he ever found it I'll never know."

CSP

"You've forgotten how little kids can get into anything anywhere. Whenever Third is around, I'm going to insist on unloading this."

He dropped the loads into his pocket, put the Cobra back in its nest.

When a prisoner with roots in Mexico breaks out of an Arizona jail he invariably runs south. When Gomez surfaced, though, it was in Tubac, 30 miles north of the border where retired Judge Monroy and his wife lived. Gomez had a shoot-out with deputies, but got away, leaving the Judge and his wife dead.

Ed Wilson and Larita were just going out the door when their phone rang and Gloria Sanchez, dispatcher at the Nogales PD said, "Chief wants you to know he's putting men around your place for security, Mr. Wilson."

Ed didn't mention it to Larita. They went on to a Shrine Club party out at Patagonia and didn't get back until late. He parked the car at the side of the house instead of putting it in the car port and walked ahead of Larita through the utility room off the patio, thinking he should have had his Cobra with him just in case Gomez had gotten in the house and was waiting for them.

Some time in the night he heard footsteps in the patio, then the utility room door being opened. He eased the Cobra from its hiding place and walked into the hall to stand in front of the utility room, the Cobra steady in his hands, chest high, FBI style.

The door opened. He did what he had to do, pulled the trigger and kept on pulling it.

When he turned on the light in the utility room he found he had fired five times at Junior.

"What happened was this," Junior explained apologetically as he, Larita, and Ed stood in the kitchen, sipping nerve-steadying tequila, "I heard about Gomez when I got home, so I decided to come down and stake out at your house for awhile. Besides, I still had your bullets in my pocket. I telephoned to see if you had remembered to reload but there was no answer. So I drove down. Your car wasn't in the car port, so I used your hideout key and came in. If I had been Juan Gomez, Dad, and you with an unloaded gun—"

"If it had been loaded they'd be calling for you in the meat wagon about now. And I would be feeling a lot worse than I do," Ed said.

Some of Gomez friends across the Line offed him shortly in some kind of drug deal, and although Third searched slyly and dililgently for it, he never found Ed Wilson's secret weapon again.

Broken Frame

Rudy Lane was a Customs Patrolman working out of Lochiel. Oley Oleson was a Forest Ranger working out of the Nogales Station. Leap Cornell was the Collector of Customs for the Arizona Collection District. Dan Carter was the U.S. attorney in Los Angeles. Fred Lavarnway, a wealthy Easterner, had a ranch in the Huachucas.

Lavarnway was a scraggly-haired scarecrow of a man who never bathed or combed his hair, wore patched Levis and dusty worn-over boots and looked like he hadn't a dime to his name. He illegally fenced a piece of government land for his own use after Oleson had advised him not to over-stock the range allotted to him. The fence was Fred Lavarnway's big-finger gesture to Oleson's friendly warning, and a usurpation of forest land that did not belong to him.

So Oleson tore down the fence, after which he and Lavarnway exchanged words, then blows, and Oleson wiped up the territory with the rancher, who tried unsuccessfully to get the Santa Cruz County Attorney to prosecute Oleson on an assault and battery charge, except that witnesses testified that Lavarnway hurled the first epithet and the first blow.

Lavarnway's scars were still not healed when Ranger Oleson began repairing fences in the Coronado National Forest in Canelo Pass between the San Rafael Valley and the Babocomari. He needed help so they sent him Bill Rickets, who had been doing odd jobs around the Nogales Ranger Station.

Rickets turned out to be a good hand, was fair company in camp, and once Oleson got used to him, he liked him. Charitably and characteristically he figured Rickets for a poor guy temporarily down on his luck, and a booze fighter.

Prohibition had recently been repealed and liquor was now available. Rickets had an old floppy-fendered Ford pickup, and every week Oleson sent him for groceries and supplies, and these outings gave Rickets a chance to unwind, although he wasn't worth much for a day after his returns.

Oleson thought it was a wonder that all the old Ford's parts clung together. It wasn't worth $20 but always seemed to get Rickets there and back safely with the goods.

There came a day, though, when Oleson sent Rickets to town that the Ford finally collapsed within walking distance from the ranger camp. It was getting on toward night, they jumped into the government car and drove to the pickup where Rickets suggested they transfer the supplies and groceries to the government car and come back for the Ford in the morning.

Oleson was transferring a heavy burlap sack from the pickup. It bumped against the side of the door of the government car and it clinked. Rancher Lavarnway and Customs Patrolman Rudy Lane stepped out of the underbrush beside the road, both with weapons in their hands.

Rickets jumped in the Ford and rattled off, and that left Oleson holding the sack literally.

The sack held 24 bottles of American Straight made in Ciudad Juarez, Chihuahua, Mexico. There were no duty-paid or Internal Revenue stamps affixed to the necks of the bottles, *prima facie*

evidence that the booze had been smuggled.

Lane and Lavarnway escorted Oleson in irons down to Nogales where he was duly flung into the slammer. He called the best lawyer in the state, Orval Winterbotham, who got him released on his own recognizance.

Oleson and Leap Cornell got together in Leap's headquarters office. In order to prove frame-up they needed the transient, Rickets, who was long gone. Not despairing, the wily old Collector used all the means available to track Rickets to L.A.

Oleson and Cornell hopped the Golden State Limited in Tucson and hurried to the Coast. Dan Carter, the U.S. Attorney, had the Marshal pick Rickets up and bring him in. He put Oleson behind a door where he could see and hear but not be seen, put Cornell at a desk and had him sorting papers with his head down so the transient would not recognize him. With masterly technique Carter subtly questioned Rickets into a corner, working him around to the framing of Oleson. By then Rickets was damp of brow and wary, his answers carefully thought out, and Carter couldn't break him.

Oleson, fuming behind the door, used a more direct method. He slammed the door open and charged out yelling, "You're a goddam liar."

So Rickets related how Lavarnway had procured the whiskey across the Line in Nogales, passed it to him over the fence somewhere near Buenos Aires Canyon, a known smuggler's route, and Rickets got the pickup to a convenient place, got Oleson, got him to transfer the whiskey to the government car.

For his part in the frame-up, Rickets was to get a bus ticket to L.A., a new white Stetson, and $100 mailed to him General Delivery.

When the smoke blew away and the fire was out, Oleson went back to Nogales with his reputation intact and got a promotion. Leap Cornell found Rudy Lane guilty of great stupidity but innocent of wrong-doing. Fred Lavarnway hired the next best lawyer in the state and got off scot-free. He decided ranching wasn't really his forte, sold out at a profit to another dude, and left for less turbulent pastures.

Rickets got a year and a day in a Federal penitentiary, which dried him out, but as far as is known, he never did get the new hat or the $100.

Pisarcik's Mistake

James Law, police chief of Nogales, hung up the phone and drove sleepily through quiet streets to City Hall in dawn's early light. At the police station he walked into the jail section where big August Pisarcik, recently retired from the Customs Service, was beginning to realize he could be in serious trouble.

"Jim," Pisarcik said earnestly, "Let me out of here. I didn't kill anyone and I didn't torch my own tool shed." He needed a shave and was in bib overalls with no shirt.

"Want to talk about it?"

Pisarcik shook his bald head stubbornly. "It's all in the police report."

Chief Law read in Patrolman T. Padilla's report that Pisarcik had heard a noise outside his house. When he walked out a man beside the door put a gun on him. Husky Pisarcik decked him, dragged him unconscious into the tool shed and put a padlock through the hasp but did not lock it for he had lost the key. When he went out after calling police the tool shade was ablaze, the padlock locked, and flames drove him back.

The report also stated that when firemen arrived on the scene Pisarcik had an empty gallon gasoline can in his hand. There was strong suspicion the body had been splashed with gasoline before the shed had been set afire.

James Law drove up Pisarcik's Hill adjacent to the border fence to view the charred remains of the tool shed. The backyard stretched into Smuggler's Gulch. So many illegals passd through it, occasionally lifting some bit of Pisarcik's property, that he took to wearing a gun and had been known to pass the word that if he caught anybody on his property again he would shoot first and ask questions later.

A badly-treated '69 VW Beetle in the yard had a U.S. Customs red seizure label pasted on the dirty windshield.

The Chief Customs Inspector, Mike Tucker, was having breakfast at the International Cafe where Law joined him. Tucker said, "Is it true Augie Pisarcik is in your jail for murder and arson?"

"It looks open and shut," James Law said. "He's not communicating."

"Stubbornest man I ever knew. At our seized car auction yesterday he paid four times what an old VW was worth rather than let a woman beat him out. Then he had to pump up two flats, juice the carburetor to get it started, and I heard it died on him before he got home."

"Who was the woman?"

"Same blonde he seized the car from just before he left the Service. He had found a baggy of pot between the engine and the firewall. The U.S. attorney said it wasn't enough for him to prosecute, the county attorney wouldn't touch it, so she walked. Big fellow with her. They stopped bidding and left Pisarcik with only sentimental value."

"Why would she want it so badly?" Law wondered.

"Beats me. Four drug-sniffing dogs say no drugs were left in it."

James Law drove back up Pisarcik's Hill, intending to make his own examination of the VW, but it was no longer there. He called in an APB on a blonde woman in a beatup grey Beetle, including a suggestion that she could be armed and dangerous. He was about to drive off the hill when his radio came alive: the VW was on Third Avenue, a street lined with junked cars and greasy garages operated by mechanics as reliable as used car salesmen. The blonde woman in it shot at Patrolman Barth, who returned her fire.

James Law drove quietly to Third, his silence made up for by the screamers on two ambulances and every emergency car in the vicinity racing to the scene. They so filled Third that by the time he got there he had to walk up from the highway intersection. They had already tossed the Beetle.

"All we came up with, Chief," said his captain, Tony Encinas, "was some grass in her purse and a little happy dust. Barth shot her, she'll live and he's just scratched."

Law drove the Beetle to the police station, followed by Captain Encinas. When the captain handed over the keys to the Chief's car, Law said: "Have somebody pour some gasoline down this bug's throat, will you, Tony?"

Pisarcik was impatient. "When do I get out of here?"

"What did you want with that old VW?" Law asked.

Pisarcik said, "I saw that woman trying to buy it back and had a feeling about it. So I bought it and left it in my yard for bait. But I went to sleep watching TV and waiting. Maybe that man would be alive now if I hadn't. She wouldn't have had to kill him to hog all of whatever's bound to be in it."

Law said, "Whatever's in it must have value. Let's go out and see."

Captain Encinas was supervising a patrolman who was washing down the concrete under and around the VW with a garden hose. A fireman stood by with a fire extinguisher.

"I think something is blocking the intake," Encinas said. "Spilled over with only half a gallon."

"That tank," Pisarcik said, "holds just enough gas to drive from

Mexico up into Third. Get me a pair of pliers, a screwdriver, and a small crescent wrench."

When these were made available to him he quickly removed the gasoline tank. It was heavy. "Hats off to whoever did this job," he said. "No wonder dogs couldn't smell it, all sealed in metal and its scent drowned in gasoline fumes"

There was another reason why the dogs had not sniffed it — they had not been trained to sniff money. The tank was neatly packed with one-hundred dollar bills.

"A sour drug deal?" Pisarcik guessed. "They took it across the Line to make a buy but the sellers never showed? So they bought a little marijuana to blow away their sorrows? Must be a half-million dollars there."

"Question," Chief Law asked. "Whose money is it now?"

"My car,"Pisarcik said, "My money. I'll fight to keep it all the way to the Supreme Court."

"Good luck," James Law said as he tossed down the bundle he was examining. "These nice tidy bills all have the same serial number."

Chinese Puzzle

In 1932 Chinese forced out of Mexico invaded Nogales, Arizona. They crossed the International Line surreptitiously on dark nights. Law enforcement officers picked some of them up loitering around town the next day. Some just walked to the police station or the border gate and gave themselves up to authorities.

They were taken to the National Guard Armory where they joined others already incarcerated. They slept in their blankets on the floor, mopped up after each of the three square meals they got each day, and pretty much took care of themselves.

The United States Government was obliged by law to return illegal aliens to their country of origin. As Mexico would not take them back, the U.S. was saddled with the responsibility for getting them off American turf. They knew they would eventually be put on a train, taken to Los Angeles, and there put on a ship for China.

The authorities at Nogles would wait until they had accumulated a number of them, then send them under escort to L.A. The escort was provided by off-duty Federal, State, county and municipal officers, and Customs Inspector Sam Raines was one of these, although he didn't speak or understand one word of Chinese.

Sam Raines was a fair-haired farm boy from Kansas, as wide as he was high, and stronger than the usual proverbial ox, noted for his stubborn and determined nature. He was seated on the steps of the Grand Avenue garita, listening to the puffing of the locomotive of the short line about to leave for Tucson, and sulking because Chief Customs Inspector Adams had turned down his request to help escort a large group of Chinese that had left yesterday when Inspector Jimmy Gleason came sauntering around the corner of the garita in his short, bow-legged steps, jerked a thumb over his shoulder, said, "I'm to relieve you, Sammy boy. Chief wants you on the double."

Wondering what trouble he might be in now, Sam trotted up to the Inspection Room in the Federal Building. The Chief hated for anyone to catch him seated behind his desk because its great size made him look as small as a ten-year old, so he was waiting impatiently, perched on one of its corners.

"Still want to go to L.A.?" he asked, biting off each word as though he hated to part with it.

"Yes, sir," Sam said, scarcely believing his good luck.

"They sent all available men yesterday to guard that group, now they need another. Go see the OIC, Immigration."

The OIC in charge was a tall, slow-talking ex-cowboy Texan named Burl Bean. He said, "One of yesterday's shipments missed the

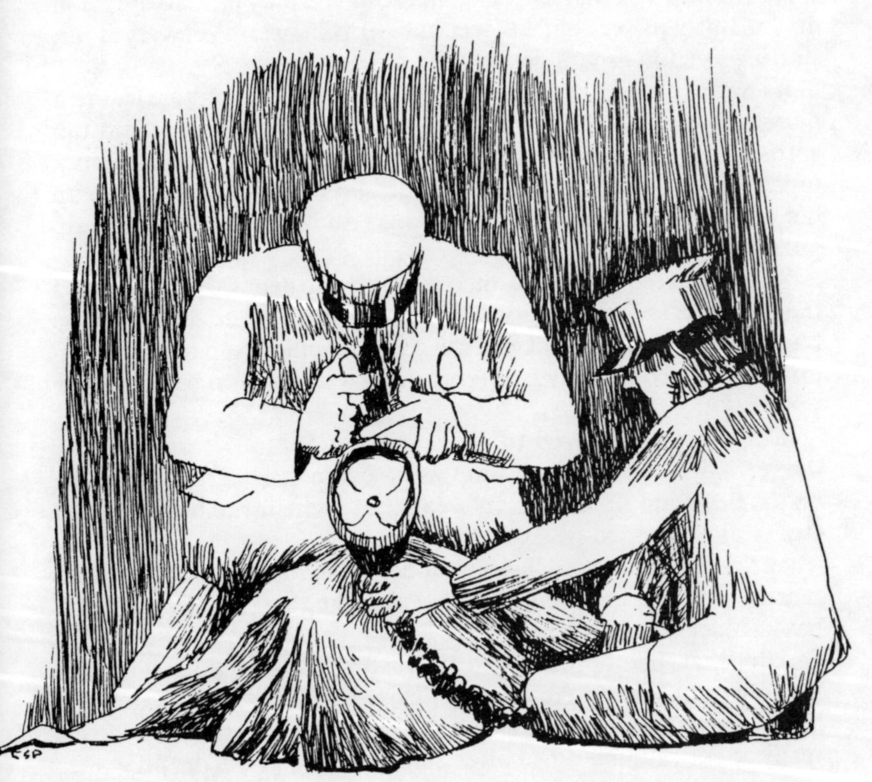

cut. He's waiting at the station. Here are his documents. Better hurry. But go by Doc Tileman's first, he's got some medicine he wants you to see that he takes."

Doc Tileman, the contract Public Health doctor, was a large red-faced man with a black stub of wet cigar protruding perpetually from the corner of his mouth like some kind of cancerous growth. He handed Sam a bottle and an eye dropper.

"He won't like these," he said, "but he has an infection that could spread. These will make his eyes smart so you may have to hold him down. But you see that he gets one drop in each eye every hour, starting as soon as you get on the train."

As Sam hurried out of the doctor's office the locomotive let out a plume of steam and a long, goodbye all aboard whistle. Sam ran across Grand Avenue, found the Chinese sitting in the shade in front of the Railway Express office, grabbed his arm and shoved him up the steps into the combination passenger and express car as the train pulled out.

Sam indicated that he wanted to apply the drops to his eyes and the Chinese submitted docilely until they took effect. Then he bucked stout Sam aside like he was a feather pillow and tried to jump off the train, complaining volubly. Sam wrestled him back into his seat.

When they transferred to the Limited at Tucson, it was time for the second round of drops, but this time Sam had to put him down on the floor and sit on him, then call the conductor to hold his head steady as Sam pried his eyes open.

At Casa Grande the Chinese suddenly sprang up out of his seat, raced down the aisle, and jumped from the train and it took Sam half-a-block to catch him.

After that, before they got to each stop. Sam would lock him in the toilet until they were moving again. Neither got much sleep on the way over to L.A. because they were either wrestling, or getting ready to, or calming down after administering of the drops.

Sam was very happy when they finally pulled into the Los Angeles depot and he could turn the Chinese over to a waiting Immigration officer, together with what was left in the bottle of eye drops.

"You'll have a hard time getting those into his eyes every hour," Sam said, "I had to fight him all the way from Tucson and I'm about wore out."

The Immigration man looked at the documents, spoke a few words in Chinese, then said, "No wonder. You got the wrong man."

The Quitter

They stood in the middle of the traffic lane, under the canopy. It was four in the morning, warm and humid, and from the north came the forbidding rumble of thunder. Frequent flashes of lightning stabbed at the surrounding mountain tops, lit up the billowing clouds. It was a night full of menace.

Newly hired temporary recruit to Customs Roy Williams said thoughtfully to Inspector Billy Cardwell: "I may not be able to handle this job I just got."

"How do you know?" asked Cardwell. "You haven't finished your first shift yet."

Williams wore a wide-brimmed grey sombrero, a clean starched khaki shirt with the collar buttoned but no tie, starched, pressed khaki pants, and the issue Colt .38 in its regulation holster glossy with shoe polish.

He looked exactly what he was, a 60-year old ex-cowboy from another era, a man who would go all the way for a friend but would take no sass from anybody.

The floor of the canyon of Nogales was flat here, and little interfered with line-of sight sound. In the distance was the explosion of a shot being fired, there was the roar of a racing engine coming their way. A siren lifted its urgent wail, and across the border the Mexican celadores came from their sleep and staggered into the street, rubbing eyes and buckling gun belts around themselves, leaving the dim recesses of their darkened low adobe garita to stare south.

Engine noise grew to a scream. High beams of headlights bounced off the white-washed walls of the buildings that lined the street, probed across the non-barrier of the border, shone far up Grand Avenue.

Bullets suddenly sang all around them, ricochets hit walls, ground, telephone poles. Billy Cardwell got behind one of the columns supporting the canopy over the traffic lane.

Roy Williams stood solid in that shower of flying lead in the middle of the traffic lane, slowly drew his revolver and leveled it down just above the on-rushing headlights. Cardwell saw his finger tighten and was about to hurl himself into that stubborn, fearless old cowboy and knock him and the gun out of the way of the speeding ton-and-a-half on wheels when the driver chickened out under the threat of that yawning revolver barrel and hit the brakes.

The car slewed sideward and stopped. Pursuing cars pulled in and stopped, irate Mexican officials flung open doors and jumped out, running forward.

Williams holstered his gun and stepped aside and motioned the car up under the inspection canopy. But as he made his move, the driver made his: hit the throttle, twisted the car straight, and made a run for it right through the narrow lane.

Above the sound of the engine, of the spinning wheels hurling gravel, his shout rang clear, "Get the hell out of the way, you silly old bastard."

Williams drew that revolver again and thumbed and triggered so fast it sounded like automatic pistol fire. But the car, flaunting red tail lights defiantly, vanished roaring down Grand Avenue toward Tucson, 65 miles away.

Chief Adams, whose home was less than a block from the Gate, strode up with his hat pulled low to the high bridge of his nose, a gun strapped around his thin waist.

"Sounded like old times," he said, his blue eyes snapping. "But I hope nobody on this Gate did any of the shooting."

Before Williams could speak, Cardwell said, "There was sure a lot of Mexican lead buzzing around here."

That afternoon Maureen awakened Cardwell. Collector Cornell was on the phone. He didn't sound happy.

"Mr. Cardwell," Leap Cornell said, "this morning you led Chief Adams to believe nobody on the graveyard shift fired at that car last night."

"That's right," Cardwell said.

The Collector said, "That's right what?"

"That's right, sir."

Cornell said, "Anyway, we brought the car back and there are only five bullet holes in it in a space no wider than my hand. If they had been a little more to the left that car never would have made it a hundred yards down the street. Only one man I know can shoot like that."

He paused. Cardwell waited. Cornell snorted, then said, "Anyway, for whatever reason, Mr. Roy Williams walked into my office a few minutes ago, laid his badge and his gun on my desk, said, 'Collector, I'm getting too old to fight, too old to run, and I'm going to wind up using this weapon on somebody I shouldn't really kill. So I quit.' "

Epilogue

These episodes deal with a time when the United States Customs Service was represented on the Mexican border by few men, mostly veterans of some war or other, life on the Line was easy with occasional flurries of excitement, once in awhile there was a seizure of liquor or taxable smoking opuim destined for the few older Chinese up in Clifton or Globe or Tucson, or a few marijuana cigarettes. An infrequent arrest.

It was an in-between time, a transition period, the changing of the guard, the discard of the rubber-stamp and paper shuffling methods in favor of the computer. The passing of a somnolent Customs Patrol from the era of boots and saddles and smuggled cattle and strayed burros to balloons in the sky and radar, fast aircraft, helicopters, speed boats, jeeps, ATVs and fast cars. Hundreds of patrol people and billion dollar budgets to combat frauds on the revenue and a deluge of drugs.

So swiftly has the "old guard" vanished from the border scene that there has been no time and no one to record events and people of the period, a lamentable gap in frontier history as significant as the passing of the cowboy, the outlaw from the southwestern scene.

Although the changes are significant, the Customs mission remains the same.

The Customs Service will celebrate 200 years of service to the nation on July 30, 1989. An Act to regulate the collection of the duties created the Service on July 30, 1789.

Time has expanded rather than altered the mission.

Part of the Department of the Treasury, the Service predates that agency by one month. It became a separate bureau in 1927, the Bureau of Customs. In August of 1973 it was renamed the U.S. Customs Service.

The background of the episodes in this book illustrates the tremendous changes that have been made, most of them during the past 15 years.

Customs:

Assesses and collects customs duties, excise taxes, fees and penalties due on imported goods.

Prevents fraud and smuggling.

Controls carriers, persons and cargo entering and departing the U.S.

Intercepts illegal high technology exports to Soviet Block nations.

Cooperates with other Federal agencies in suppressing the traffic in illicit narcotics and pornography.

Enforces reporting requirements of the Bank Secrecy Act.

Protects the American public by enforcing auto safety and emission control standards, flammable fabric restrictions, annual and plant quarantine requirements.

Protects U.S. business and labor by enforcing regulations dealing with copyrights, trademarks, and quotas.

As the principal border enforcement agency of the United States, Customs enforces some 400 provisions of law on behalf of more than 40 Federal agencies.

The Commissioner of Customs is appointed by the Secretary of the Treasury. Customs headquarters is in Washington, D.C. It is organized into five major offices, each headed by an Assistant Commissioner. The offices are: enforcement, inspection and control, commercial operations, international affairs, and internal affairs. The Controller of Customs oversees administration.

The Chief Counsel, an arm of the General counsel of the Treasury Department, advises the commissioner on legal matters.

Today, 45 districts and areas with 300 ports of entry are supervised by seven Regional Commissoners. Overseas, U.S. Customs maintains offices in U.S. embassies and consulates in Bangkog, Dublin, Hong Kong, London, Mexico City, Ottawa, Paris, Rome, Tokyo, Seoul, Panama City, Vienna and The Hague. An attache represents U.S. Customs in the U.S. Mission to the European Communities in Brussels.

The Nogales District is in the Southwest Customs Region with headquarters in Houston, Texas. The District, headed by a District Director located in Nogales, still has the border crossings it had during the period covered by these episodes, with the exception of Lochiel. The Regional Intelligence Branch maintains substantial data in computerized data cases directly accessible to field units. These data include car and marine lookout files (a long way from the piece of paper most Inspectors in earlier times carried in their cap), a daily seizure log with historic seizure information.

In the view of this writer, the "good old days" as described in the 50 episodes in this book will never come around again. This book and its sequel are their swan song.

Translations

These translations are for words commonly used along the border and may have other meanings as well. As they are words used in everyday conversation by both Mexicans and Americans and thus a part of the border idiom, only the first appearance in the text is italicized.

abrazo .. ritual hug and handshake

adobe .... sun-dried building block

aficionado ..... fan (of a sport, for example)

aftosa .... hoof and mouth disease

alambrista .... illegal entrant, "wire jumper"

alcalde .... mayor

arroyo.................... a gully

Asi es la vida. .... That's life.

bacanora .... bootleg mescal

bandido .... bandit

barberia .... barber shop

basura.................... trash

birria....... cooked beef, shredded

botana .. free lunch, hors d'oeuvres

bulla .... noisy

burro .... donkey

cabron .... big male goat, an insult

cajuama .... turtle meat

Camino de muerte........ Road of death

cantina .... saloon

cantinero .... bartender, saloon-keeper

cargadores .... porters

Cara de caballo .... Horse face

Cara de mapa .... Map face

carne de res .... beef meat

celador .. Mexican Customs guards

chapo .... short, shorty

chi-chi................... breast

condones .... condoms

Coronel .... Colonel

coyote....... dog-like wild animal

culo.................. buttocks

curios .. souvenir-type merchandise

domperos .... trash pickers at a landfill

Donde nacio?..... Where were you born?

dorado .... a gold-colored fish

El Camino del Diablo...... Devil's Road

El Colorado ....the red-haired man

Estado Mayor ...... General Staff

fayuquera ...a pack-rat smuggler of small items, female rooster

gallo ....rooster

ganga .... bargain

garita ....guardhouse

gringo ....North American

groseros .... rude, discourteous people

guajalote .... turkey

honcho .... boss

huero ....a light-skinned, blue-eyed man

la bola ....short for "la bola de la vida", The ball of Life, accumulation of years, old age

La Caverna ..... Popular Nogales, Sonoran. restaurant

La situacion hace el ladron. ... The situation makes the thief.

libre .... free

limon .... lime fruit

Lleva frutas o plantas? .... Got any fruit or plants?

machismo .... vigorous masculinity

maquila .....twin plant operations

mariachis .... band of brass and strings

marijuana........pot, weed, grass, Mary Jane

mescal..... product of a step in the making of tequila

mesquite .... a desert tree

mojado ..... wet, an illegal entrant

mordida .... the "bite" - a tip given to facilitate service

muy contento........ feeling good

nada .... nothing

Oso Negro .... Black Bear — a popular brand of alcoholic beverages

peso ......Mexican monetary unit

petaca............trunk (of a car)

petate .... reed mat

Pimeria Alta ....part of the Gadsden Purchase

pinto ...... a "paint" horse, brown and white

pistola......applied to either pistol or revolver

por supuesto .... of course

puta .... prostitute

Que trae? .... What are you bringing?

quelites de las aguas .. amarinth — a pigweed that induces hay fever, comes after first summer rains. Good cooked like spinach, fried, or raw in salads

rapido........fast. As used herein, the train from Mexico City to Nogales

siesta..............afternoon nap

sin embargo ....nevertheless

sombrero .... hat

sotol ......Product of a step in the making of tequila

Tengo que mirar la petaca........ I have to look in the trunk.

tequila, tequilitas .... Mexican alcoholic beverage made from the agave

tierra........... one's home land

tomateros ...... anybody who had anything to do with the buying and selling of tomatoes from Mexico

trago .. a swallow, meaning a drink of something alcoholic

tranvia .... a jitney bus

tripas de leche ..... small intestines

turistas ..... tourists, also diarrhea

uno por uno.......... one by one

vaquero .... cowboy

Viva el Presidente! ... long live the President!

Books from Golden West Publishers

The Other Mexico—Revel in ancient treasures and modern pleasures with world traveler E. J. Guarino, your host to the myriad museums and archaeological ruins in today's Mexico. 90 full-color photographs, plus maps, site-plans, index. (176 pages)...***$9.00***

Cowboy Country Cartoons—a cartoon excursion through the whimsical west of renowned cowboy cartoonist-sculptor Jim Willoughby. Western humor at its ribald best! (128 pages)...***$4.50***

Southwestern frontier tales more thrilling than fiction. Trimble brings history to life with humor, pathos and irony of pioneer lives: territorial politics, bungled burglaries, shady deals, frontier lawmen, fighting editors, Baron of Arizona, horse and buggy doctors, etc. ***In Old Arizona*** by Marshall Trimble (160 pages)...***$5.00***

Southwest Saga—the way it really was, by Southwest historian-journalism William C. McGaw—Esteban's life among the Zuni, Pancho Villa's raid north of the border, Mark Twain's drug scheme, the strange death of Ambrose Bierce, etc. (160 pages)...***$5.00***

Ride the back trails with modern-day mountain men, as they preserve the memory of Arizona's rugged adventurers of the past. Buckskin-clad, the mountain men stage annual treks from Williams, AZ all the way to Phoenix, AZ and to other destinations. Hilarious anecdotes of hard-riding men. ***Bill Williams Mountain Men*** by Thomas E. Way (128 pages)...***$5.00***

Books from Golden West Publishers

Men played for keeps in the Arizona Territory . . . where romance of stagecoach routes was interrupted by murder from ambush . . . where raiding was a way of life . . . where ranchers and rustlers had scores to settle . . . place names that still ring with vibrant memories of a glorious past . . . recaptured for all time in the pages of ***Old West Adventures in Arizona*** by Charles D. Lauer (160 pages) . . . $5.00

Discover arrowheads, old coins, bottles, fossil beds, old forts, petroglyphs, ruins, lava tubes, waterfalls, ice caves, cliff dwellings and other Arizona wonders. Detailed maps and text invite you to vist 60 hidden, out-of-the way places. ***Explore Arizona!*** by Rick Harris (128 pages) . . . $5.00

Visit the silver cities of Arizona's golden past with this prize-winning reporter-photographer. Come along to the towns whose heydays were once wild and wicked! Crumbling adobe walls, old mines, cemeteries, cabins and castles. ***Ghosts Towns and Historical Haunts in Arizona*** by Thelma Heatwole (144 pages) . . . $4.50

The saga of centuries-old search for Spanish gold and the Lost Dutchman Mine continues. Facts, myths and legends of fabled Superstition Mountains told by a geologist who was there. Mysteries of lost hopes, lost lives—lost gold! ***Fool's Gold*** by Robert Sikorsky (144 pages) . . . $5.00

The American cowboy had a way with words! Lingo of the American West, captured in 2000 phrases and expressions—colorful, humorous, earthy, raunchy! Includes horse and cattle terms, rodeo talk, barb wire names, cattle brands. ***Cowboy Slang*** by "Frosty" Potter, illustrated by Ron Scofield (128 pages) . . . $5.00

ORDER BLANK

Golden West Publishers

4113 N. Longview Ave. Phoenix, AZ 85014

Please ship the following books:

_____ Arizona Adventure ($5.00)
_____ Arizona Cook Book ($3.50)
_____ Arizona Hideaways ($4.50)
_____ Arizona—Off the Beaten Path ($4.50)
_____ Arizona Outdoor Guide ($5.00)
_____ Bill Williams Mountain Men ($5.00)
_____ California Favorites Cook Book ($3.50)
_____ Chili-Lovers' Cook Book ($3.50)
_____ Citrus Recipes ($3.50)
_____ Conflict at the Border ($5.00)
_____ Cook's Book, The ($5.00)
_____ Cowboy Country Cartoons ($4.50)
_____ Cowboy Slang ($5.00)
_____ Easy Recipes for the Traveling Cook ($5.00)
_____ Easy Recipes for Wild Game ($6.50)
_____ Explore Arizona ($5.00)
_____ Fools' Gold ($5.00)
_____ Ghost Towns in Arizona ($4.50)
_____ Ginger Hutton. . .from the Heart ($5.00)
_____ How to Succeed Selling Real Estate ($3.50)
_____ In Old Arizona ($5.00)
_____ Joy of Muffins ($5.00)
_____ Mexican Desserts ($6.50)
_____ Mexican Family Favorites Cook Book ($5.00)
_____ Old West Adventures in Arizona ($5.00)
_____ Other Mexico, The ($9.00)
_____ On the Arizona Road ($5.00)
_____ Pecan-Lovers' Cook Book ($5.00)
_____ Prehistoric Arizona ($5.00)
_____ Southwest Saga ($5.00)
_____ Sphinx Ranch Date Recipes ($5.00)

CONFLICT at the BORDER
—true tales of a U.S. Customs border officer!
by Charles S. Park

Enclosed is $__________ (including $1 PER ORDER for postage and handling)

____
(NAME)

____
(ADDRESS)

____
(CITY) (STATE) (ZIP)

This order blank may be photo-copied.